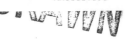

MW00587690

JUN − − 2023

Praise for *Cry, Baby: Why Our Tears Matter*

"*Cry, Baby* is an honest, powerful, and critically important book about what we transform with our tears—and how making space for our tears can transform us and the society in which we live. This book forges new cultural pathways by way of the bold, brave, naked open heart."

—Rabbi Danya Ruttenberg, author of *On Repentance and Repair*

"Alternatively tender, sharp, and funny, *Cry, Baby* speaks beautifully to the power our tears carry, how they can transform both people and culture. The attention to crying's social dimensions—how our ability to weep is shaped by racism, patriarchy, homophobia, and other forces—make it particularly timely. A gift to all who cry, and all who long to."

—Simran Jeet Singh, bestselling author of *The Light We Give*

"With the precision of an anthropologist, Benjamin Perry delicately and beautifully explores the significance of a good cry. I'm so grateful to Benjamin for asking these questions. I'm so grateful to *Cry, Baby* for answering them. Or at least inviting us to ask the same questions for ourselves."

—Dylan Marron, author of *Conversations with People Who Hate Me*

"I've often laughed until I've wept, and I have sometimes wept myself into giggles, but *Cry, Baby* made me so very aware physiologically, psychologically, and spiritually of the what, how, and why of the beauty and urgency of tears. With the precision of a journalist, the passion of a prophet, and a proven history of delicious prose, Benjamin Perry takes us on a healing journey that includes his own. Together we taste and see the power of embracing our tears, of watering the seeds of our dreams for a healed and whole world with our crying so they sprout justice, peace, and love."

—Rev. Dr. Jacqui Lewis, author of *Fierce Love*

"I am profoundly struck by Benjamin Perry's *Cry, Baby*. It explores the heart of what it is to be human in the form of our tears. I found it incredibly moving and helpful for understanding and metabolizing my own grief. Required reading for a more empathetic society."

—Lindsey Boylan, political activist

"This book drew me in right away because it's about our sacred human journey. What does it mean to cry? What does it mean to come home to ourselves in a culture that teaches us to disconnect from our very souls? *Cry, Baby* is a guide to embodiment, full of rich stories and important questions about how we exist in this world and what it takes, not just to notice and name our grief, but to move through it and allow it to change us. This is a book about reclaiming our sacred humanity through our sacred tears, and healing ourselves, one another, and Mother Earth along the way. What a gift Benjamin Perry has given us; I hope you'll accept it."

—Kaitlin Curtice, award-winning author
of *Native* and *Living Resistance*

Cry,
Baby

Cry, Baby

Why Our Tears Matter

BENJAMIN PERRY

Broadleaf Books
Minneapolis

CRY, BABY
Why Our Tears Matter

Unless otherwise noted, Scripture quotations are taken from New Revised Standard Version Bible, copyright © 1989 the Division of Christian Education of the National Council of the Churches of Christ in the United States of America. Used by permission. All rights reserved.

Excerpt from J. Mase III's "Josephine" from *The Black Trans Prayer Book*, edited by J. Mase III and Dane Figueroa Edidi. Reprinted by permission of author.

Excerpt from "What Do You Do with the Mad That You Feel?" and "Sometimes I Wonder Whether I'm a Mistake," reprinted by permission of Fred Rogers Productions.

Cover image: Timmary/Shutterstock
Cover design: Patrick Sullivan

Print ISBN: 978-1-5064-8511-9
eBook ISBN: 978-1-5064-8512-6

Printed in Canada

For Erin, who helped me find my tears.
This book wouldn't exist without you
and, in significant ways, neither would I.

CONTENTS

CHAPTER 1

Learning to Cry

I can't remember when I stopped crying. I never woke and decided, "No more tears for me!" There was no pivotal moment, no traumatic incident in which I wept openly, was gruesomely mocked, and swore off tears forever. Yet by my early twenties, as surely as if I had cauterized my tear ducts, I hadn't wept in years.

If I wrote this about any other crucial biological process, that statement would be remarkable. Imagine opening a book by saying, "I haven't pooped since Bush was president," or "It's been a decade since last I sneezed." Such a confession would be headline news, or at the very least you'd suggest I consult a doctor. But *not* crying is not only unremarkable; it's oddly normative. Obviously, defecation is somewhat more crucial to our continued survival. However, the degree to which you might be shaking your head and scoffing at the comparison bespeaks how we've denigrated crying to something that's quotidian at best and, at worst, shameful.

Life begins with tears. And while few would desire sobbing with infant-like frequency, daily weeping is far nearer to our natural state. How freely children cry, and with such minimal provocation. Growing up, I cried often. I was a rough-and-tumble youngster, so a number of these episodes were brought on by the thousand natural shocks of childhood bumps and scrapes. But kids possess more complex interior lives than we give them credit for, and many of my tears were incited by the kinds of emotional harm with which adults are acquainted. I remember sobbing at the unfairness of school, the ways that institutions weren't always attentive to my needs and desires. Loneliness was another frequent cause, sometimes rooted in actual estrangement from my peers and other times in my own perception. But that's the funny thing about crying: our tears do not need to be grounded in empirically provable sorrow for them to be valid. If we are attentive to them, we will learn something about ourselves, each other, and the world in which we live.

When I was eight, recess descended into chaos. A small wood adjoined the soccer field of the school I attended, and some of my friends spent a couple weeks building a wondrous little fort there. But I was one of those kids who found destruction far more alluring, and so I gathered a crew of other kids to knock down what my friends had made. Thus began a few weeks of cyclical desecration and rebirth: painstaking craftsmanship with sticks and leaves crumbling beneath an onslaught of little sneakered feet. It all came to a head when my friend Josh, the fort's original architect, got so enraged that he disinvited me from his birthday party. He had a pool, so little could be more tragic. I remember weeping bitterly the night of the party as I languished at home.

It's tempting to admonish a crying child, "It's just a party; there will be others." And honestly, having repeatedly destroyed what my friends had made, what did I think would happen? All that is valid. There would be more parties, and I had absolutely brought this suffering upon myself. Yet to reflect on this moment from such a coolly detached vantage point misses what was happening. Amid those tears, I learned crucial things about myself and the world: I knew more deeply the value of relationships, and I better sensed how fragile our social webbing can be. And in that anger and frustration, I also understood the consequences of my actions better than any parental lecture could impart. That wasn't the last time I destroyed something beautiful, but it began to unravel my fascination with destruction for its own sake.

In contrast, when I was twenty, I broke up with a girlfriend while utterly dry-eyed. She wept copiously, but I felt next to nothing. It wasn't because I didn't care about her; I was genuinely upset at her distress. But in the twelve years between these stories, something inside me had hardened. Whereas I cried profusely over smashing a makeshift fort, I was now able to destroy a months-long relationship without a single tear. In the moment, I didn't even realize how profoundly disturbing this transformation was. It had become normal to skim above the surface of my feelings, letting myself see the broad outline of my emotions but never risking confrontation with their depths.

When I decided to attend seminary a couple years later, I told people it was to "find myself." That frame suggests I yearned to forge a new identity, discover my future. But in fact, I went to seminary in large part because I yearned for a more honest and authentic emotional life. I longed to fix what had been deadened, and to reclaim the breadth of humanity I had somehow lost.

I'll never forget the class that set me on the road to reclaim my tears. We were talking about the destruction of the temple as we read Lamentations, a book in the Hebrew Bible, what

Christians sometimes call the Old Testament. To help us explore the unimaginable grief the Israelites experienced in exile, our professor broke us into groups and asked us to share with one another the last time we wept (a true seminary assignment if ever I've heard one). One by one, my classmates talked about moments of deep grief.

When my turn came, I was speechless. I racked my brain, but I truly couldn't think of the last time tears had even graced my eyes, let alone when I sobbed in earnest. I can't recall what I mumbled. But I remember sitting at the table with a potent sense that I had lost something along the way—something fundamental.

I resolved to find it. So I rushed home after class, determined to spur tears by any means necessary. And thus I embarked upon a truly absurd afternoon. I watched videos of dogs reunited with owners after years-long separation. I threw on a tearjerker movie. I recalled how it felt when I was bullied as a child, hoping some personal trauma might unlock the floodgates.

Nothing.

I looked up videos of parents telling their gay kids how much they loved them. I set mood music. I read a letter from my Gran in which she told me how deeply she cared for me.

Nothing.

After several hours I was exhausted and beyond frustrated. It began to feel like so much emotional masturbation in a body unable to climax. I began to despair that I might never cry again.

Finally, I did the most extreme thing that I could imagine. I thought about my parents, how deeply I loved them, and then I pictured them dying. For some minutes, I closed my eyes, and imagined them on their deathbeds. I thought about all the things I would say, and what might be left unsaid. All of a sudden I noticed my cheeks were wet. It was like a threshold had been breached, and I began to sob uncontrollably. Years of numbness crumbled into a cavalcade of tears. I had done it: I had abused myself into crying. And it was terrific.

To be clear, I was a mess. There's that beautiful stereotype we see in movies: a single tear, meandering down the cheek, scored by a solemn sniffle. And while some people may cry like that, it sure isn't me. My body heaved with sobs, and my nose became a blubbering mess. Tears flowed uncontrollably, to the point where I began to worry they might never stop. And even when they did, I lay on my bed completely spent and exhausted. I was like a man who hadn't run in years who had inexplicably attempted a marathon. But I felt alive.

The next morning, I embarked on some more absolute lunacy—the kind of emotional extremism to which seminarians are wont. I decided to cry every day. I would approach weeping as a spiritual discipline, I decided, greeting it with the same fervent dedication I devoted to my morning prayers or my burgeoning meditation practice. Every day after my classes were over, before I gathered with friends to study or hang out, I would sit down and will myself to tears.

In the beginning, I had to delve into imagine-dead-parents kinds of pain to prime the pump. I'd watch videos of refugees talking about the homes they left behind, their fragile dreams for the future. I listened to stories of harrowing abuse or watched heartrending short films like *Changing Batteries*. Each time I'd find the path toward tears a little better worn, discovering the physical and emotional responses that point in their direction. I leaned into the catch in my throat, the shortening of breath, and I became more and more adept at coaxing my body to feel deeply.

Within a month or two, I experienced a curious transformation. Many days, my crying practice was no longer necessary. I was now crying regularly, and with much less provocation. A classmate would tell a moving story, and the tears would well up. Witnessing small acts of kindness was now enough to blur my vision, and listening to gorgeous music in a church service was enough to make me weep. The intentional habit of crying had recalibrated my emotional baseline. My body now regularly found the emotional release that, just months ago, it took hours of conscious effort to provoke. And as I let myself embrace the tears that now steadily fell, I felt more like myself than I had in years.

Emotional numbness is sneaky: you don't realize how much you've closed yourself off until you begin to feel again. It had become normal for me to witness pain, anguish, beauty, love, and ecstasy with detached indifference, or else with the simulacra of each emotion. I could experience broad contours, but they were all nearer to my resting state than any heightened sensation. I'd watch shadows flicker on the walls of my heart and make myself believe they were real.

That's the thing about suppressing tears: you can't just wall yourself off from sadness, because emotional tears run the full spectrum of our feelings. Humans cry when we feel deep joy or when we're overcome with pride and admiration for someone we love. Our eyes brim before the awesome or majestic—in moments of mystical ecstasy when we feel oceanic communion with nature or a crowd. We cry from longing *and* when we're reunited with what we long for. And there's no reliable way to isolate and eliminate just one of these emotions. To staunch our tears, we must deaden ourselves to the world.

We who have chosen to discard weeping—or been forced to—walk around like ghosts. We are afraid to fully live.

This is not a book about how to teach yourself to cry—although if you learn to cry while you're reading it, I'll consider it a success. It's not even an apologetic for tears—although if it convinces you of the worth of our weeping, I've done my job. It is an exploration, an invitation to curiosity, and a hope that by encountering the myriad ways tears act as a prism that refracts our humanity, you will be brought closer to your own.

When I set out to write a book on crying, I had no idea how neatly the history of my tears and their absence would map onto my own personal development. The decade I lost my tears was when I, myself, was most lost. Conversely, the path toward reclaiming my authentic self from a hardened artifice was watered with them. The following years dramatically changed my own emotional life. But if tears had *only* done that, I probably wouldn't be an evangelist for crying, and I certainly wouldn't be writing this book. I set out on the journey to fix something broken inside myself. What I didn't anticipate were all the ways that tears would bring me into deeper relationship with a world that's breaking.

The life of a minister extends a peculiar invitation to a host of intimate and tender moments. I've cried with parents while their child lay dying, with friends as I've joyfully married them, on the streets in protest, and in quiet moments of desolation looking for my own hope so I could offer some to others. The person I've become is inextricable from that weeping.

Before I began researching this book, I thought about tears as a consequence: the emotional sum of previous experiences, evidence of the past cascading down our cheeks. Now, however, I think about tears as a doorway: an invitation to be fully human, in all the complexity that entails. Crying is not always an exclamation point that marks the end of growth or an emotional change; it can be an ellipsis that beckons us toward a more complete life.

Being human is not neat and tidy. Crying is messy too: ragged gasps, copious snot, shattered voices trembling to articulate the enormity of our emotions. It's fitting that people say they "break down into tears," because the experience of weeping can certainly leave us feeling split apart, disassembled. And yet, paradoxically, it can be tremendously clarifying, lending new insight and even seeding dreams. To talk about tears honestly, we must embrace these contradictions.

The dry-eyed stoicism that once infected me is actually a symptom of cultural illness. Together we will explore in these pages why humanity developed the proclivity to shed emotional tears, the benefits of that kind of weeping, and the way embracing this capacity offers both personal and social healing. We'll explore physiological and psychological research about crying and the role it plays in our development. And we'll see both secular and sacred literature testify to how crying invites transformation. We'll examine a variety of social forces that inhibit our tears and how that harms both individuals and communities. Finally, we'll imagine what a world that wholeheartedly embraces weeping would look like, inspired by those who are already embodying that change. Along the way, you'll meet a variety of folks who will describe how tears, and their absence, have shaped them.

I want to avoid the convenient narratives we often build around tears, the ways we try to deodorize an act that does not need to be prettified. We'll look at the many facets of crying, the ways that tears are strung between a variety of different biological, psychological, and social forces. I make no claims to exhaustively encapsulate every form of tears. All books are written within a particular context. As I write this, more than a million Americans have died from COVID-19. Hundreds of thousands of these neighbors did not have to die but were sacrificed in a rush for

8

"normalcy." I began drafting in the middle of the Delta wave and am finishing as Omicron rips its way across the country. Because of these circumstances, tears of grief hold outsized sway in these pages, while tears of joy and laughter do not nearly receive their due. For this I apologize. But I am writing what I know. I very much hope that someone else will write a book about euphoric tears; I look forward to reading it.

Similarly, I do not catalogue every cultural context that informs when, how, and if we feel safe and comfortable crying—and what those tears yield—because there are as many of these as there are people. No one cries in a vacuum. How does white supremacy stifle tears? How does enforcing a gender binary mold the universal tendency to weep? How has patriarchy established boundaries around "acceptable" and "unacceptable" kinds of tears? How is that suppression also an expression of internalized homophobia? These questions and more intersect our identities, creating a unique matrix into which our tears fall. I have interviewed a wide range of folks—from prominent theologians to actors, teachers to TikTok stars—to elucidate broader experiences than the ones I carry in my own body. Yet even after dozens of interviews, I frequently come across some new detail or dimension I haven't heard before. Crying is an intimate and particular act. At the same time, I hear seemingly universal themes about people's relationships with their tears—even from folks who come from widely divergent backgrounds and experiences. It is those commonalities, most of all, that I hope shine through.

More than anything, I've tried to be honest. Crying is never just about crying. And crying is never more harmful than when it's wielded to deceive. But when we let our tears strip away the illusions we construct, we know ourselves and each other more deeply. So I offer truth as I have seen it, no more, no less. And

I'm profoundly grateful for anyone who finds themselves in these pages.

Weeping is simultaneously one of our most private acts and most social, essential for forging connection. There's nothing more intimate than sobbing alone—except when our tears land on someone else's shoulder. And when they fall in concert with others' tears, we exponentially magnify their power. Collective weeping knits our heart with our neighbors'. Tears let us know a stranger more deeply than words ever could. They offer comfort in moments when we are beyond consolation, and they can even stoke revolution.

Some years ago I found myself packed into a van as part of a peace fellowship delegation, driving across the country to offer our solidarity at Standing Rock. Watching Indigenous leaders bare their grief as a testament to the government's inhumanity is a lesson in tears that I'll never forget. But it was also a stark reminder of the limitations of what we are able to offer someone as they are grieving.

I made a pilgrimage to that sacred encampment because my heart was breaking watching folks proclaim "*Mni Wiconi.* Water is life!" to people who answered with tear gas and rubber bullets, and I wanted to Make A Difference.™ So I spoke with an editor and proposed an article. I fully intended to write a fiery report on the deep immorality of our hunger for oil. But when I arrived at the windswept North Dakota plains, I discovered I was there with the wrong intentions. Confronting grief helped me find better ones.

The night before we arrived, police had sprayed water protectors with firehoses in the bitter winter. What a vicious irony, wielding ice and hypothermia against elders naming the river's sacredness. Greeting tears with weaponized water is a cruel, inhumane act.

The mood in camp when we arrived was dire. In addition to using firehoses, police had also lobbed flash-bang grenades into the crowd, blowing off a woman's arm. Whatever reasons that sent me lay shattered by stark reality: I was not going to save anyone. And if that was why I was there, I would only make things worse.

So instead of trying to conduct interviews to flesh out a narrative I crafted in the van, I decided to simply listen to anyone who would speak with me, to sit and be present. I heard stories of generational trauma, of wounds that yawned across the convenient lies we present as history. I listened to Native youth talk about older generations' pain and the fierce conviction they inherited to defend what is theirs.

Over and over again, what I heard most acutely was deep grief. We were there over Thanksgiving, and one man I spoke with put it clearly: "There was never Thanksgiving for us. Only Thankstaking." Tristen, a Payómkawichum fifth-grade teacher, was similarly blunt: "They're trying to poison our water and land, and take away our culture. People are getting teargassed and shot for praying." That kind of trauma and sorrow isn't something any one person can fix. But it's something to which we can be present. Listening and crying next to someone doesn't solve centuries of harm, but it doesn't do nothing, either.

And we can sit beside someone else's grief by listening with our hands. Anyone who has comforted someone who's mourning knows that sometimes cooking them dinner says more than our words are able. So the other way I tried to be present to overwhelming grief and anger was chopping a seemingly endless pile of wood. For a few days, I let my arms offer their insufficient atonement. Each crack of the maul became its own aching, anguished cry.

That was a story about grief I witnessed. It's easier to talk about other people's tears than it is to sit amid our own. To hide behind others' crying without being honest about ours betrays the vulnerability tears demand and deserve. And it's simpler to tell you about that time I wept as a spiritual experiment, because that story still places me firmly in control. To hide behind one's own past can be a bypass all its own.

So I'll be honest: on December 5, 2020, I began a season of weeping that's still ongoing, as I watched the church I love and serve burn to the ground.

By the time I awoke that Saturday morning, I already had a couple dozen missed calls, texts, and voicemails. I opened one from my boss, the Rev. Dr. Jacqui Lewis. Her voice was anguished and clipped: "Ben, the church is on fire. Call me when you get this." At first, those words sounded absurd, like she had called to say, "Ben, my giraffe has got loose," or "Ben, this orange has typhus."

That's the thing about churches: their majesty belies their fragility. Imposing stone walls and breathtaking wood inlay suggest they'll live forever, safely outside the ravages of tragedy and time. So when the words "The church is on fire" finally sank in, my next thought was, "Oh, there's a small fire in the parish hall." So I quickly googled *Middle Church Fire*, and promptly sat down on my bedroom floor. Because what I saw instead was an inferno.

Flames exploded through the windows and licked the roof like locusts. The blaze was so intense it lit up the night into an incandescent dawn. As I watched, I was suddenly aware that I was crying. I began to sob, not in controlled, disciplined tears but full-body heaves. I wept, and the church burned. It felt like watching a friend die in real time.

And so began the strangest day of my life. I continued to sob uncontrollably, yet I desperately needed to work. An inbox full of press requests and a congregation in crisis would not permit what I yearned for—to wrap myself in a blanket and cry until dehydration. So I cried as I wrote media statements. I cried while we organized a vigil. I cried over my keyboard and into my phone. And in the occasional quiet moment, I cried with my coworkers. Because the church still smoldered, and there was nothing we could do to resurrect its body.

When you're sobbing, it feels like the world should stop on its axis and the sun should freeze in the sky. Raw grief grips us by the shoulders. Yet there is small mercy in tasks that need to be completed. Labor can offer mild distraction. But as anyone who has busied themselves organizing a funeral knows, this does not buy escape from pain; it just puts that sorrow on layaway. I awoke the following Friday, and I realized, in mild panic, that there was nothing more to do. After a stretch of twelve-hour workdays, a day off loomed ahead, terrifying in its expanse. I made a pot of coffee but forgot to pour a cup. By the time it finished brewing, my lacrimal glands had supplanted my frontal cortex, firmly in control. I began, in the Mountain Goats' words, to "walk the house like a little boy lost in the mall," until the walls themselves felt threatening. I fled, in vain hope that my anguish might stay home behind me.

We had recently moved to Maine, and I still didn't know anyone, but I also couldn't handle another minute alone. My partner, Erin, was back in New York visiting family, and there's only so much crying we can do by ourselves before we begin to feel slightly mad. So I drove to town and wandered into a store. There I was immediately reminded of another reason we cry: it connects us to community, even when we don't yet have one.

The owner, Ariel, greeted me as I walked in. She asked me how I was doing, and all my polite lies collapsed around me. "Actually, pretty bad," I admitted. I started to cry, softly, and she offered me a beer. So there we sat at 11:00 a.m. on a Friday morning in an empty boutique, Modelo in hand.

I told her about why I loved Middle Church so deeply: how it was a safe haven for queer people, the first place so many folks heard that God loved them, exactly as they are. I talked about its fervent antiracism, the ways that Jacqui and the congregation shattered the perverse union between American Christianity and white supremacy. I spoke of the love that echoed in those stone walls—exuberant hugs and gospel hymns that reverberated in the sanctuary long after the choir left.

Ariel tenderly listened to my grief. And then, after I had told her the story, her reply was as blunt as it was compassionate: "Wow, that fucking sucks."

For days, I had sat through well-intentioned people telling me, "It's okay, the church isn't a building; the church is a people." While I know that's theologically true, when you're crying amid the ashes of an immolated church, those words feel less like kindness than a reminder of all you've lost. Ariel didn't try to fix that grief. She didn't offer paltry condolences. Instead, she named the calamity.

Never underestimate the power of cheap beer and truth plainly spoken. That afternoon was the first I didn't spend weeping; my pain was named and known. I imagine my words alone would have spurred her compassion. But tears communicate something speech cannot.

Crying is a conduit that tethers our soul to another; it circumvents our intellectual processing of someone else's pain. It's why even the most calloused people still react when someone cries in their presence. They may denigrate or disregard the pain, but rarely do they act as if nothing is happening. We are hardwired to respond to crying—it's at the very core of who we are.

The omnipresence of crying throughout art, myth, and sacred literature reflects tears' centrality in our collective life. And, as we'll see in chapter 2, this isn't coincidental: we are physiologically and psychologically hardwired to shed emotional tears. The cultural efforts to quash them will always be ineffective at best, because there's only so much you can do to suppress people's humanity. We continue to weep in grief, because weeping tells us something fundamental about what we are called to do in our short time on this planet.

Crying brings clarity, for through our tears we see what truly matters: our connection to one another, the deep mutuality that is both our birthright and responsibility. A culture that mourns better can help to build a world where no one is forced to mourn needlessly. But our lacrimation doesn't just help us communicate; it whispers secrets about ourselves—our fervent hopes and aching longing.

Reclaiming our right to cry not only cares for our own bodies; it helps us prophetically reimagine culture. This duality is what makes crying so powerful, and it's why pernicious social forces try so hard to stop it.

Crying can change both our bodies and our environment. A neuropsychology professor once told me, "There's no such thing as a psychological change that happens all by itself." Every shift in our psyche is linked to underlying anatomical and social alterations. If our tears facilitate change, there must be a reason why.

CHAPTER 2

This Is Your Brain on Tears

One summer in my early twenties I was vacationing with my family, and after the beach heat, we took a dip in a nearby pond. But as we walked up the wooden stairs to leave, the serenity was shattered by a horrendous crash and blood-curdling screams. I sprinted up the rest of the steps and saw absolute chaos. Someone had crashed their truck and a woman had become pinned between her vehicle and a car the truck had struck. She howled in pain and fear.

Quickly, I and another half-dozen folks leaped into action. We circled the back of her car to move it just enough to free her from that metal grip. As we approached, I saw something that absolutely broke me: her daughter was in the back seat, banging her fists on the window, pleading for her mother. She couldn't have been more than five or six, and her eyes were wide and brimming with terror. Slowly, we were able to lift the car and free her mom, and the paramedics soon arrived and tended to her and her daughter. Everyone was fine, and all the onlookers gradually dispersed and went about their day.

As we were driving away, I looked at my palms and realized the undercarriage of the car we lifted had left a couple nasty slices. When we got back to the house, my grandmother put some Epsom salts in a basin and told me to soak my hands. As soon as my fingers hit the water, I began to weep uncontrollably. It wasn't the pain from cuts that prompted my tears, though. All I could see when I closed my eyes was the daughter in the backseat, screaming for her mom. Quietly, Gran rubbed my back as I sobbed.

Finally, after some time, the tears passed. My breath gradually returned from ragged gasps, and my heartbeat slowed. The horror of the previous hours faded slightly into sepia tones, and I was able to get ready for dinner. Still, the girl in the backseat remained seared into my vision. Even years later, as the rest of the memory fades, her anguish remains vivid. It's as if the tears I shed remembering her pain etched her across my cortex. I still think about her from time to time. She's probably in high school now, and I hope she's doing well.

So what function did my tears serve? Grandpappy Darwin is clear: our bodies did not develop by accident. Evolution finely tuned our biological systems, maximizing our ability to adapt, survive, and thrive. Crying is no exception. Something about my wracking sobs helped me to recover from the vicarious trauma of that ill-fated afternoon while also connecting me to strangers I'll never see again.

"My tears have been my food, day and night," the psalmist writes, creating a rather startling image. Unless you're embarking on an eccentric and ill-fated new diet, tears as food is clearly metaphorical. Yet physiological and psychological research suggests that emotional tears—psychogenic lacrimation, if you want to get technical—nourish our minds and bodies in ways that surpass common understanding. The relief we feel after crying is not an illusion, nor is the way it knits us to our neighbors. What if our tears are actually crucial to both individual and social development? And, if that's true, how does suppressing tears inhibit flourishing?

What if crying actually feeds us?

We cry for a variety of reasons. First and foremost, tears are necessary to care for our eyes. Each time we blink, our eyes are coated by secretions from our lacrimal glands, to prevent our eyeballs from drying out. But they moisten in response to external stimuli as well. When the air is smoky, our tears provide a protective layer to shut out possible contaminants. We also shed tears in response to chemicals in the air, as anyone who has chopped onions knows. Or, as is ever so popular on the internet, we cry when *it's just so dusty in here.*

For the purposes of this book, we're going to ignore most of the basic physiological facts about tears. That choice feels a touch churlish, as we should all be deeply grateful for how our eyes care for us, in a hundred wondrous, quotidian ways. But if I begin going on about the interplay between tears and allergens, I fear you may cast this weird little treatise in the nearest dumpster. So we're going to focus in this chapter less on the physiological realities of our tears and more on why we cry in response to intense emotion.

Although still a nascent field of study, research on human tears suggests that emotional tears did not develop by accident. A good place to start is understanding that crying is deeply tied to our parasympathetic nervous system, and that crying helps to calm and restore our body to homeostasis after a period of arousal. This explains why, although we may cry *during* periods of heightened stress, more often we begin to cry *after* a crisis has passed, as our heart rate and breathing slows. Many people I interviewed talked about what seems, on the surface, to be a counterintuitive phenomenon: they wouldn't cry while they were visiting a dying friend, for example, but would break down after they left. While they likely wanted to "stay strong" for their loved one, research suggests underlying biology is at play too.

Paradoxically, however, research suggests that the act of crying also *increases* sympathetic nervous system activity, which is the system that feeds somatic arousal. Studies that measured participants' reactions to emotional films found that their heart rates remained steady in the minute immediately preceding tears but significantly increased while they were sobbing. So even though crying's onset often accompanies recovery from heightened stress, once tears begin, we experience an echo, of sorts—a reverberation in our nervous system of the crisis that just passed. In some significant way, our bodies are physically returned to that initial distress. Many people report feelings of clarity after an intense bout of weeping. Our bodies are offering us a gift: an opportunity to process that intense emotional experience in a hopefully safer setting.

One can imagine how this was evolutionarily adaptive. If you're fleeing a predator, midsprint in your escape is probably a poor time to begin weeping. Yet if you simply moved on from the experience, you wouldn't have the opportunity to review the period that immediately preceded the attack. Crying afterward, in a safe location, may have afforded early humans the chance to process that trauma and hopefully take action to avoid it in the future. So while it's inconvenient to break down in a Walmart parking lot after ending a relationship in the electronics section, we can be grateful for how our bodies help us revisit that pain to prevent its recurrence. (Don't date men who wear fedoras; it won't end well.)

Interestingly, Darwin himself famously believed that emotional crying served no physiological purpose. He saw it as a simple byproduct of mechanisms designed to keep the eye lubricated and protected from outside irritants. In *The Emotional Expression of Man and Animals*, he puts this conclusion bluntly: "We must look at weeping as an incidental result, as purposeless as the secretion of tears from a blow outside the eye, or as a sneeze from the retina being affected by a bright light." And because science has not dramatically improved its understanding of the reason behind our tears, many researchers' descriptions of crying still appear to operate within that Darwinian frame.

So why is there so little research on emotional crying? Why do we know so little about our tears?

Emotional crying is a notoriously difficult phenomenon to study. Scientists Ad J. J. M. Vingerhoets and Rudolph R. Cornelius note a stark gap between public consensus that crying is beneficial for physical health and what researchers have been able to document. One study of articles about crying published in popular magazines from the mid-1800s to 1985 found 94 percent of the articles recommended readers embrace their weeping as a crucial tool for relieving tension. This consensus runs parallel to historic advice from medical practitioners. As early as 1694, Dutch physician Franciscus Mercurius Von Helmont wrote about "the necessity of crying after bereavement in order to prevent the development of distemper or sickness." Famed

British doctor Sir Henry Maudsley suggests a causal relationship even more plainly: "Sorrows which find no vent in tears may soon make other organs weep."

Despite this broad and longstanding agreement between medicine and popular science, however, researchers have been largely unable to find evidence that crying is good for physical health—nor that inhibiting tears is damaging. Reliably provoking emotional tears in a laboratory setting is more difficult than stimulating other biological processes such as sweating or salivation. Indeed, the laboratory setting itself may be part of the problem; being invited to weep under researchers' patient gaze may itself hinder real emotion. Most researchers studying emotional crying show participants a sad film and cross their fingers that it's sad enough. It's difficult to think of a better method, but it's also hard to suppress the feeling that this artificiality may not paint a full picture. And because emotional triggers vary wildly from person to person, most studies report that a substantial portion of participants don't cry at all—which likely creates its own selection bias. Most of what we know about crying from physiological research includes results only from people who can cry when watching a sad movie in a lab.

And the number of researchers who even attempt to study tears is relatively small. When I spoke with Dr. William Frey, one of the first scientists to research tears, he told me he had great difficulty in securing grant funding for his crying studies. The lack of subsequent clinical applications, and the absence of diseases or abnormalities to warrant immediate investigation, make it hard to justify any kind of substantial investment in the field. So while the origin and purpose of our tears have a long history in poets' minds, those questions have more modest footprints in psychological journals.

Isolating crying as an independent variable when it comes to something as huge and complicated as someone's overarching physical health is also problematic. Consider someone who cries every day. The frequency of their tears tells you very little. Are their daily tears a healthy coping mechanism that helps them process the pain they carry and the stress of the world? Or are they crying because they're absolutely overwhelmed and on the brink of total collapse? Further complicating the matter is the fact that, at different points in our lives or even a month, we may be both of these people. Plus, comparing tears' effects across different people introduces all kinds of confounding variables. One very healthy person may cry frequently because they're in tune with their emotions. Another may shed tears with equal frequency out of frustration with their chronic health conditions. Averaging the two will yield muddled results about the relationship between health and crying.

Moreover, studies that do overtly compare crying and physical health often simply take a snapshot of people's health at one moment in time and compare that against self-reported data on how frequently they cry. Imagine, for example, that our hypothetical patient in the previous paragraph—the one who cries frequently and suffers from chronic illness—had enrolled in that study. Their presence would pull the data in a direction that suggests crying frequently harms physical health. But what if this person had started weeping frequently in the previous year, and the ensuing emotional relief had actually *decreased* the severity of their symptoms? Research designs that compare crying and health at a fixed point in time have no way of measuring that kind of complexity. Sadly, no one has done the kind of longitudinal studies that would help us tease apart the relationship between crying and physical health.

Anecdotally, we know that tears frequently provide a path for people to move through pain and grief. In Joan Didion's tragic and beautiful book about the death of her husband, *The Year of Magical Thinking*, she describes how her immediate reaction to his death was a detached numbness. (One doctor at the hospital describes her as a "cool customer.") "I do not remember crying that night," she writes. The waves of grief only started, she reports, "seven or eight hours after the fact, when I awoke in the apartment." The tears help her confront the truth—her husband is dead—even as they move beside a parallel refusal to concede that reality. "I needed to be alone," she writes, "so that he could come back."

Tears help Didion travel from the realm of magical thinking to the reality of what she has lost. It's something that chaplains, therapists, and clergy—those who are familiar with people's emotional responses to loss—know all too well. When I ask Rabbi Michael Adam Latz about this dynamic, his response is blunt: "What I find in my rabbinic practice is that people who do not weep do not grieve well. Folks who do not cry in hard moments have a substantially harder time dealing with their grief."

An absence of psychological research doesn't mean that science tells us nothing about how tears affect our well-being. It just means that we may need to come at this question through other means, by reviewing the effects of crying we *do* know about—ones that are easier to study.

Consider the following thought experiment: you're walking through the train station, killing time before your departure, when you see someone sitting alone on the steps. The person on the stairs looks sad; they are looking at the ground, and their brow is furrowed. As you keep walking, you see another person, sitting on a bench, sobbing. Their shoulders are shaking, and tears are streaming down their face. Who are you more likely to approach to inquire if they're all right?

Recent research has focused on the interpersonal benefits of crying. Researchers describe in *Evolutionary Psychology* how "tears have contributed and stimulated our empathic abilities and large-scale mutual collaboration with non-kin and strangers." In one study, scientists showed participants a variety of photographs of sad and neutral faces. In the experimental group, researchers digitally added tears to the sad faces, to provide an additional visual cue that the person in the photograph was experiencing distress. They then measured the speed and accuracy with which the observer was able to recognize anguish. While participants were reliably able to identify sad faces without the presence of tears, when they saw someone crying, they were significantly faster to respond.

The scientists then repeated the experiment but instead measured the degree to which participants thought the person in the photograph needed support. Reliably, subjects reported that the crying people needed more support than their dry-eyed counterparts. Considering both experiments together, researchers suggest that "even at an early pre-attentive level, tears already can be detected and serve as an important visual cue which speeds up subsequent recognition." Someone else's tears communicate to the viewer a need for social assistance.

It's easy to see why this would be evolutionarily advantageous. Put simply: humans are not physically remarkable animals. We're not particularly fast, nor particularly strong. We lack the fangs or claws that help other species defend themselves, and instead of a hard exoskeleton we have soft, fleshy exteriors, vulnerable to the elements and physical trauma alike. And unlike the young of most other creatures, our children take years before they develop any kind of self-sufficiency, remaining wholly dependent on care-givers for food and protection.

We *are* truly remarkable, however, in our ability to communi-cate our needs to one another, and in the ways we form mutually beneficial relationships beyond our immediate kin. In our ex-ample of walking through a train station, your willingness to help a stranger is the product of this evolutionary superpower. Crying is a potent signal that something is wrong. It allows us to share, at a glance, that we need help. And it also stimulates in others the *desire* to help, to comfort, and to soothe. This also explains why young children are so fast to cry, and why that ability develops far more quickly than our capacity to communicate with language. Additionally, theorists propose that emotional tears may persist in older children as a "silent strategy to elicit needed support from specific individuals most likely to provide the desired assis-tance." In a study of the neurobiology of crying, Lauren Bylsma and her coauthors write that it is "superior to an acoustic signal," which would not only attract caregivers but predators as well.

The tears we shed that are rooted in emotional responses have a higher protein content than tears we cry in response to physical stimuli, such as those shed while cutting an onion or walking through a field of ragweed. We'll look at that fact more in a bit. For now, what's interesting, as Heather Christie writes in *The Crying Book*, is that some scientists suggest we evolved a higher protein content in emotional tears "because it increases their viscosity, slows the rate at which they fall, increasing the chance they will be seen and their message received." Crucially, though, the benefits of this process are reciprocal. When we offer care to someone, we feel closer to them afterward. Our emotional connection serves as both a benefit of prosocial relationships and a stimulation for future interpersonal support.

If you read the research on crying, you'll find a curious dismissal of the social aspects of tears, as if having a communicative function somehow makes them less biologically essential. It's a pretext that motivates Dr. William Frey in his work: part of the impetus for his quest to uncover the biological function of tears is a conviction that something so innately woven into our physiological systems wouldn't be serving a purely interpersonal function. After all, he points out, "other animals clearly communicate their needs and wants with expressive body language and by crying with whines, whimpers, yelps and screeches without tears." And while we'll get into why I think he's right, we do ourselves a disservice as a species if we treat the social aspects of crying as if they were unimportant.

Crying, quite literally, prevents us from dying before we develop the capacity for language. Infants use tears to communicate a wide array of basic requirements—from biological imperatives, like the need to eat or be cleaned after pooping, to an emotional desire to be held. Crying is babies' primary means to alert caregivers to a need, and while a baby's tears are not always a life or death matter, they can be. This, alone, is a crucial act. Frankly, anything that helps us not die should probably be regarded as more than an eccentricity.

But there's also copious evidence that tears' usefulness surpasses mere survival. Infants whose cries are ignored, for example, can suffer a wide array of attachment disorders in later childhood and adolescence. To become healthy, well-functioning adults, we must learn early that our distress will elicit empathy, support, and care from our parents or caregivers. While the consequences are more severe if crying is ignored in infancy than later in childhood or youth, no evidence suggests that this essential relationship between tears and soliciting aid from our environment simply vanishes when language develops.

A distinct sign of this enduring relationship between crying and securing assistance is its cultural universality. If the link between adult crying and securing assistance were not biologically innate, people in some parts of the world—but not others—would offer assistance to criers. Research, however, shows that no matter where they live, people are more likely to offer help when they see someone crying. In one study of more than seven thousand people across forty-one countries and six continents, participants were shown pictures of faces with or without digitally added tears. They were then asked to rate how much they felt drawn to offer that person assistance. Researchers in every single country reported that tears significantly increased people's likelihood to help. (If you're curious, the effect of the added tears was smallest in South Korea and greatest in the United Arab Emirates. So if you're going to cry in a train station, do it in the UAE.)

We can communicate that we need support through salt water leaking out of our eyes: this might seem like a trite or insignificant observation, but it is truly radical. Even more remarkable is the fact that this communicative effort can reliably make other people—even ones we don't know—more likely to provide it! The human ability to expand our tribe—to widen our circle beyond those few people who share a biological incentive to ensure our genes are passed on—has few analogues in the natural world. It is what has allowed humans to develop exponentially more complex social bonds than those of other creatures. And while processes like language and religious belief are more responsible than tears for this robust extratribal growth, we fool ourselves if we believe nonverbal communication doesn't play a significant moderating role. And tears aren't just another nonverbal exchange. They affect our emotional lives in ways a meaningful glance or hand gesture never could.

Consider our proclivity to cry when we see someone else crying. These contagious or empathic tears are an outward manifestation of an inward kindness. How beautiful it is that our bodies are wired to spill care that words alone cannot express. If you've ever cried next to someone, you know that it can create an understanding that transcends language. When you cry empathic tears, instead of simply saying, "I feel your pain," you have taken some of that anguish into your own body. It may not reduce the sorrow the other person is experiencing, but it makes both you and them feel less alone. That is not a blessing that should be taken lightly. The feeling of being seen for who we are and what we are experiencing is humanizing in the fullest sense of the word.

Perhaps story is a better vehicle than data for uncovering the truth behind our tears. Qualitative studies often portray tears in richer detail than quantitative analyses. In one, researcher Hans Ladegaard examined eighty-nine "crying events" at a volunteer shelter for foreign domestic workers in Hong Kong. The tears he describes weren't shed because a researcher played *Brian's Song* while observing college students through a one-way mirror; they flowed naturally as workers reported harrowing tales of abuse they experienced that forced them to flee for safety. In this context, we see a side of crying too often absent from sterile clinical depictions. "Some of the women, who were quiet before telling their story and who cried continuously as they took us through their traumas, became notably more vocal after they had cried," Ladegaard reports. The social benefits of tears lie not just in the ways they change how others treat us; tears change us, too.

Weeping beside others affirms that the pain we have experienced is real. It can unlock our ability to control our own narratives and change our own futures.

In June 2018, I traveled with a delegation of faith leaders to McCallen, Texas, to report on the horrors of the Trump administration's family separation policy. When we arrived, we visited Catholic Charities of the Rio Grande Valley, the first destination for many migrant families when they're released from US detention centers. The heat was sweltering, the kind of punishing, claustrophobic haze that tries to suppress even your breath. Through the scorched glimmer rising from the asphalt, we watched dozens of parents approach surrounded by their children, carrying the ones too young to walk.

As the faith leaders in our delegation spread around the center to talk with migrants, bearing witness to the stories of government abuse, I began to play with a small child, the normalcy of plastic trucks in sharp contrast with our deeply unnatural surroundings. As I played and chatted with Edwin, his mother came over. I asked in my rough, conversational Spanish if I could interview her for my article; she agreed and we began to talk. But I stopped asking questions when I noticed she was crying. Her tears rolled gently—not a loud ostentatious cry, but soft and gentle, perhaps a mixture of relief at being safe for now mingling with anxiety about the journey ahead. For a moment we cried together.

I can't pretend to know what Maria's tears did for her, and whether they helped her carry the immense weight of the journey. From her words, I learned about Maria's journey from Honduras and the circumstances under which she sought asylum. But from her tears, I learned the deep wound of our border better than any words I could write, then or now.

Social scientists can debate whether there's enough evidence to prove that tears provoke emotional catharsis. Yet it's difficult to have an encounter like the one I had with Maria and reach any other conclusion. Data only takes us so far, and parsing p-values like tea leaves feels very much like an exercise in missing the point when we consider the testimony of Janet, one of the folks at Ladegaard's shelter. "Crying is good for the heart," she says, "because if we don't cry, we explode."

A cardiologist could object and ask Janet to pinpoint the precise mechanism by which inhibiting tears could provoke coronary collapse. But I doubt anyone except the most calloused observer would find that objection compelling. When scientists are unable to explain people's widely reported intuition that crying is cathartic, research methods may be a more logical culprit than mass public deception.

Yesterday I sobbed in my room as I read about the extinction of the ivory-billed woodpecker. I started reading an article about how logging had decimated their habitat, exterminating the beautiful bird by the mid-1940s. I gazed at photos of their black and white plumage, and all of a sudden I was filled with overwhelming sorrow about the violence we inflict—a majestic beauty that evolved over millions of years had been eradicated in a few hundred. Before I knew it, I was undone. You'd be hard pressed to identify any interpersonal purpose for *these* tears—other than perhaps communicating to any neighbors who overheard that I was not a Stable Adult™ equipped to handle this world.

I jest, but we all know that sometimes it is *precisely* when we're alone that we often dissolve into self-salination. The frequency with which people weep by themselves when losing a job, ending a relationship, or recalling past trauma suggests that tears do not only serve social functions.

One possible explanation for solitary tears is that crying is a self-soothing behavior, a form of emotional regulation that helps us mitigate painful feelings we wish would go away. This rationale is so ancient and pervasive that even mentioning it feels like stating the obvious. As early as ancient Rome, the poet Ovid observed, "It is some relief to weep; grief is satisfied and carried off by tears." Despite longstanding belief that tears attenuate sorrow, however, many of the early laboratory studies examining this relationship rejected the hypothesis. A 1988 study found no positive effects of crying, and likewise Randall Martin and Susan Labott found "no support for the view that crying improves mood." So what gives? Are we fooling ourselves that tears are cathartic?

In an elegantly designed 2015 study, scientists helped to explain the gap between laboratory findings that crying harms our mood and widespread anecdotal reports that crying improves it. Similar to other researchers, they showed participants a sad movie to elicit tears and then compared the moods of folks who cried during the film against those who did not. As in other studies, feelings of distress significantly increased for criers while tears were flowing and in their immediate aftermath, while noncriers did not report a change. However, when researchers followed up, they found "strong mood improvement experienced by those participants who cried," which made people feel better than they did before the experiment. Likewise, more granular research comparing crying frequency across personality type has found that, regardless of individual differences in personality, "on average, emotional crying was followed by more positive affect and less arousal, pointing at a potential cathartic effect."

Yet while science has begun to confirm what people have long known to be true, it does not yet explain *why* crying is cathartic. One fascinating hypothesis suggests that tears are a marker of a psychological change. Dr. Matthew Pelowski wondered what makes some people cry when they react to a piece of art, while others do not. Crying, he argues in his papers, is a product of a cognitive or emotional journey between our previous expectations and the need to confront reality. So, for example, if I'm watching *Old Yeller* (because I've made some spectacularly poor viewing choices), as I watch Travis and Yeller bond, I expect that the two will enjoy a long and happy life together. Then, when Yeller is bitten by the wolf and shows symptoms of rabies, even as I *know* what may be coming, part of me resists conceding these new and fundamentally intolerable circumstances. And I'm not just focused on a story about a boy and his dog; I'm also reflecting on unexpected, tragic losses in my own life, reluctant to confront them.

Finally, when Travis is forced to shoot his beloved companion, I cry because, in Pelowski's words, I have "given up attempts at overt control, eventually confronting and changing [my] own schema or expectations." I no longer maintain hope in that beautiful future I imagined; my tears are the product of that concession. And hopefully this encounter in a fictional world also helps me accept my own circumstances. Crying in this model does not manifest purely in the event itself, but through a larger process as we "experience disappearance of a barrier, solution to a problem, or transformation of a previously held worldview."

Wanting more information, I called Dr. Pelowski to ask him some questions. Pelowski is vibrant and energetic, and his passion for the way crying can change us radiates across the call. I was curious about how one decides to study crying, and he told me that art, not tears, was his entry point. He studied painting as an undergrad, but he became more engrossed by effects art has on its observer than producing it himself. He remembers, for example, reading about people weeping in a Mark Rothko exhibit. "It was fascinating to me that Rothko's art was making people cry," Pelowski says. Rothko's paintings are abstract, mostly composed of large blocks of luminous color. "Why would that ever happen?" Pelowski asks. "If it does happen, it has to be 'in your head.'" This phenomenon was his first inkling that crying was about more than its immediate stimulus. "The literature on crying is moving away from [an understanding that's] purely overwhelming emotion," he says. "Maybe that's part of it, but it's cognitive too. It's this process you go through. The tears are a byproduct of getting to a certain point in your dealing with the world."

A process-oriented approach, Pelowksi says, helps us understand why people may cry during an aesthetic encounter—looking at a piece of art, listening to music, or reading a book. "Art walks a really interesting line," he explains. "You can tell yourself that you can enter this space and leave the implications at the door, that you'll walk out the other side and maybe the world will be the same as you left it." People let their guard down when they approach a painting or film in ways that they wouldn't at the grocery store, he points out, expecting that "everything will be okay—and then suddenly it's not okay."

When we feel like crying, we have a choice. We can either process what we're experiencing and let the tears fall, or we can avoid these emotions, dispelling them with humor or repressing them entirely. "Repressing is super unhealthy—it leads to heart disease, and cancer, and all sorts of things," Pelowski tells me in our conversation. But it's not just physical ailment we risk when

we hold back the tears; we also miss the opportunity to be transformed. You sacrifice a "learning opportunity," Pelowski laments.
Not crying is "a way of not letting the world get too close."

It sounds extreme to link emotional repression to something
as dramatic as heart disease, and it's tempting to conclude that
this is a correlative and not a causative relationship. But some crying research points toward crying playing a more essential role in
maintaining physiological well-being.

In his seminal book *Crying: The Mystery of Tears*, Dr. William H.
Frey summarizes a series of studies his team conducted examining emotional tears' chemical composition. The news-grabbing
headline from their study was that, compared to tears prompted
by an irritant in the eye, "the protein concentration of emotional
tears was 21% higher." Specifically, Frey reported that the hor-
mones prolactin and adrenocorticotropic hormone (ACTH) and
the endorphine leucine-enkephalin were found in much higher
concentrations than they were in other parts of the body. The
presence of ACTH is of particular note, because it's a very reliable stress indicator. Outside the kidney, no other body part is
known to concentrate proteins *above* the levels at which they're
present in the bloodstream. On the basis of these results Frey
hypothesized that crying may actually be one process by which
the body excretes the byproducts of stress, to help return our
system to homeostasis.

To date, very little research has been done to investigate
whether crying might serve the kind of excretory function Frey
hypothesized. One study measured levels of cortisol in the saliva
of sixty-three women after watching a sad movie, and found that
the stress hormone decreased most in women who cried most
intensely. Further studies have not attempted to confirm these
results, however, and it's unwise to declare anything conclusive

from a single study. Yet we can't ignore the fact that people report feeling better after they cry.

If tears do serve an excretory function—if they do, in a real way, detoxify our bodies—it could help explain why people who never cry can seem so, well, toxic. Hopefully researchers will continue to investigate the relationship between tears and toxins. For now, we're left with tantalizing possibilities.

That summer day, when the woman became pinned between the car and the truck in the parking lot, her tearful cries drew a crowd, which helped to save her. But man, that car was heavy! I sometimes wonder if it was her tears, and her daughter's, that made the difference. I'm sure we would have lifted the car eventually, but I can't tell you how seeing her daughter banging on the window, eyes awash with fear, quickened my muscles. I persisted in helping to free that stranger even as the undercarriage bit into my palms because in that moment, I would have done anything in my power to make that little girl feel safe and protected, to assure her everything would be all right.

That kind of extreme adrenaline wreaks havoc on the body. Even after the moment itself had passed, my heart was racing, my breath was shallow, and my brain kept reliving what I witnessed again and again. Put simply: I was out of control. That evening as I started to cry, some of those physiological symptoms intensified. My breath came in ragged gasps, and I have no doubt my pulse rose.

But even as I continued weeping, I could feel my parasympathetic nervous system springing into action. While tears cascaded down my cheeks, my breath grew even. A calm descended, returning my body to a preaccident homeostasis.

After my sobs subsided, I was no longer the same person I had been before the crash. Something about the experience had changed me. I felt connected to these total strangers, convicted by a fundamental sense that their well-being was intertwined with my own. It was as if our shared experience tethered our lives with tough yet tender thread.

We didn't evolve to meet this many different people. In the prehistoric environment, it's highly unlikely that I would have had this extremely intense emotional encounter and then never see the woman and her daughter again. The connection between us, facilitated by our tears, would have helped us survive. More than sheer survival, these tears invite our thriving.

CHAPTER 3

Sob Stories and Transformation

Once upon a time there was a girl who cried with such reckless abandon that she nearly drowned. I'm not talking about the titular character in Nine Days' top 10 single "Absolutely (Story of a Girl)," who engulfed the world with her tears—seemingly well within her rights after her boyfriend promises she'll be lovable when she's smiling. I am, instead, referring to *Alice in Wonderland.*

In Lewis Carroll's timeless classic, Alice very nearly doesn't make it into Wonderland at all. Upon eating a cake and becoming far too large to enter the doorway, she weeps a veritable sea of tears. After a subsequent shrinking, she finds herself literally awash in her sadness. "I wish I hadn't cried so much," she exclaims. "I shall be punished for it now, I suppose, by being drowned in my own tears! That *will* be a queer thing, to be sure!" (Modern readers are permitted a wry chuckle that being consumed by one's tears is a very queer thing, indeed.) In the middle of this self-induced peril, however, a mouse passes by her distress. In a sentiment familiar to anyone who's cried so profusely they fear they may be simply carried away, she calls out, "O Mouse, do you know the way out of this pool? I am very tired of swimming about here, O Mouse!" Thus, she is saved.

Curiouser and curiouser: if you pay attention to how tears manifest in literature and life, this pattern repeats itself again and again—crying precedes moments of transformation. This salty morass is the admission Alice must pay to traverse the boundary between this world and limitless imagination. She is literally displaced: tumbling from the table, she is forced to overcome her feelings of helplessness. By swimming through her despondency, she can reach the wonders that lie beyond. In Carroll's book, this encounter creates a bridge between Alice's dissatisfaction with Victorian manners in the first chapter and the adventure that is to come. In life, the scene points to a deeper truth that manifests in popular and sacred literature alike: when we cry, we create the circumstances that can foster dramatic change.

The more we attune ourselves to how crying shows up in literature, sacred texts, and myth, the more we see the pattern: crying is part of change. In the narratives that shape us, tears often function as a lubricant for transformation. There's a curious paradox, for example, in Octavia Butler's *Parable of the Sower*. The novel takes place in a near-future America ravaged by climate change and political instability (set in the year 2024, it feels rather uncomfortably close to home). The protagonist, Lauren Olamina, is born with a form of hyperempathy: she literally experiences others' pain and pleasure in her own body. If she watches someone get shot, it's as if the bullet pierced her skin. Much of the story follows Lauren from one calamity to the next, as she wanders the wastelands, gathering a community around her and looking for a home. Despite her physiological connection to the pain around her, however, her eyes remain dry the entire book.

Even as she witnesses her family's murders, the only tears that dot the page are the readers'.

In the sequel, however, Lauren cries multiple times. In *Parable of the Talents*, Lauren has now married and gathered a sizable commune around her, living off the land in northern California. In this apocalyptic future, wealthy towns now run as autonomous enclaves, with their own private security, food cultivation, and governance to separate them from the desperation of those beyond their massive walls. Lauren has become pregnant, and her husband receives an offer to live and work in a nearby safe haven. It would offer unparalleled stability for her daughter but require them to leave the community they'd been cultivating in the wild.

Despite the allure of safety, Lauren chooses to stay and risk everything to nourish a dangerous love instead of accepting a seductive cage. In that moment of decision, she begins to weep. "I did cry then," Butler writes. "I sat there with tears running down my face. I couldn't stop. . . . After a moment, I decided I was where I wanted to be." This woman who has both watched loved ones die and killed others in self-defense, all with unstained cheeks, finally breaks down. Making space for these emotions finally allows Lauren to confront her destiny and seize her calling. She decides to commit herself to Earthseed, the post-Christian faith she created to guide her community, which she longs to spread beyond its walls.

She cries a second time after a murderous band of Christian nationalists destroy her commune, steal their children, and enslave the adults—calling it salvation. Lauren and the members of her community endure savage beatings, rape, and unending humiliation for years as they devise a plan to escape. Eventually, the members of her community choose their moment, kill their captors, and seize their freedom. "We wept ourselves to sleep like tired children," Lauren writes in her journal. In the morning when they wake, she sends her followers away to spread the values of their community and transform the world.

And Lauren weeps one final time. After searching for each other for decades, Lauren and Larkin, her stolen daughter, are reunited. Larkin had been placed into a Christian nationalist foster family to be indoctrinated, and while she has shed some of the poison they fed her, Larkin is also wary and distrustful of a mother who she sees as more committed to her nascent church than she ever was to her family. When they finally meet, Lauren, now an old woman, invites Larkin to move in and form a life together. Larkin says no, and Lauren retreats behind a saline veil. In her tears, she understands that there was nothing she could have said that would make Larkin stay; her daughter was already gone.

Together, these three crying episodes punctuate pivotal moments that draw Lauren from being a traumatized woman, beholden to herself and her small community, toward her future as the mother of a movement. This calling is not without cost: she abandons the small, safe future she might have had—cozy, privileged domesticity with her husband and child—for an opportunity to change the fundamentally broken systems that would have surrounded that life. After her initial community is destroyed, she again finds herself at a crossroads. Reeling in the wake of that devastation, she could have been forgiven for clinging to the ashes of what she lost. Instead, Lauren leaves what is burned, placing her faith in a resurrection far grander than any comfort she might find clustered by that tomb. Finally, in her confrontation with her daughter, Lauren comes to terms with what she has sacrificed. She owns the human cost of becoming a prophet. In each crying jaunt, tears cut through comfortable lies that might have anesthetized Lauren from what she truly wanted, watering the truth she herself proclaims: "God is change." Tears are not just a *product* of having made the choice; they are a part of the choosing.

But tears are not only part of the calling of fictional prophets like Lauren Olamina. Crying shows up, again and again, in our stories about real-life prophets too. Buddhism, Hinduism, Islam, Judaism, Christianity: these religions and more all prominently feature stories of people struggling to accept the ways that a higher truth has claimed them. Frequently, religious prophets' tears carve space within them to live into who they are becoming. Like a river that cuts into canyon walls over millennia, their weeping creates its own contours into which they will pour their lives.

One of my favorite parts of the Bible is the story of Joseph. Having been introduced to a trans reading of this ancient Hebrew text, I now can't see it any other way, so that's the emphasis I'll hold in this retelling. And my deep thanks goes to to J. Mase III, coeditor of the *The Black Trans Prayer Book*, for this perspective.

Jo is Jacob's favorite child—the one who can do no wrong in their father's eyes. As a sign of that affection Jacob, thrilled and delighted, tells Jo to ask for anything they want. Jo gleefully requests a beautiful dress. The Hebrew words *k'tonet passim*, often translated "coat of many colors," are used only one other place in the Bible: 2 Samuel 13, in which the phrase describes a princess's gown.

As if their father's favor and a ballgown weren't enough, Jo is also given prophetic visions by God, blessed with ability to discern the future. They share the fruits of this talent with their brothers, who immediately become enraged. The brothers lure Jo out into the wilderness, beat them, strip them, and throw them in a well. These jealous, vengeful siblings then sell Jo to a band of passing enslavers, rub blood all over the radiant dress, and tell Jacob that Jo must have been eaten by wild animals. While other prophets in Scripture are often called to their work through water or smoke, Jo is baptized in their own blood, shed for the crime of wanting to be beautiful. There's no explicit mention of tears in this section of the biblical text, but Jo must have shed them while huddled in a camp with their enslavers, naked, bruised, and battered. You can imagine that a different person, after being assaulted for telling others their visions, would disavow that gift and renounce that power. But Jo doesn't let trauma steal what God bestowed. Somewhere in that weeping, Jo affirms their prophetic calling, because they continue interpreting dreams.

Here we must condense a longer story. Jo is sold into slavery in Egypt, where they use this ability to become the Pharaoh's chief advisor. After foretelling seven years of plenty followed by seven years of famine, Jo is appointed by Pharaoh to oversee grain distribution for the entire kingdom. As abundance turns to hunger, people begin to travel to Egypt from surrounding nations, in hopes they might be fed. Among these travelers are Jo's brothers, who journey to Egypt from Canaan. When they arrive, they do not recognize Jo, but Jo immediately sees and remembers the ones who left them for dead. Jo questions them harshly, and in the course of this interrogation their brother Reuben expresses his remorse and anguish at the violence committed against Jo. "Didn't I tell you not to sin against them?" Reuben exclaims. "But you wouldn't listen! Now we must give an accounting for their blood."

Here, then, is where the Bible *does* explicitly record Jo's crying. Jo leaves the room and begins to weep, lamenting relationships that have been shattered and the profoundly mixed emotions that greet a chance to mend them. Jo emerges with a tentative hope that this encounter might begin to heal this deep well of hurt. But they are, unsurprisingly, still suspicious—not ready to simply forgive that pain with open arms. So they devise a plan—a test of their siblings' trust. They seize one of the brothers, Simeon, and send the rest back to Egypt with instructions to return with their youngest brother, Benjamin. It's a classic traumatized response—Jo still yearns to reconnect with their family but cannot rebuild that bridge without assurance that it will not be torched again. When their brothers return with Benjamin, however, Jo is overwhelmed by emotion. "Deeply moved at the sight of their brother, Joseph hurried out and looked for a place to weep," the story says. "So they went into a private room and wept there." As Genesis 45:2 says in the New Revised Standard Version, Jo "wept so loudly that the Egyptians heard . . . and the household of Pharaoh heard about it."

It is in this second bout of weeping that Jo devises a plan to reveal themselves to their brothers. The story gets a little convoluted, so I won't go through all the details, but eventually they are convinced that it's safe enough to show themselves. And in that moment, to quote J. Mase's poem "Josephine,"

> *love broke through*
> *the darkness of resentment*
> *And for the first time*
> *your family saw you*
> *as you*
> *as Magnificent*
> *for it was your word*
> *that saved them from starvation.*

These crying episodes are not incidental details. They arrive at pivotal moments of transformation, and the tears themselves are transformative. They resurrect a relationship between Jo and their brothers in ways that the brothers' actions alone never could. Crucially, this story is an excellent parable for forgiveness: it places the onus of repairing the relationship on the shoulders of those who fractured it while granting control for the entire process to the person who was harmed. Tears usher Jo through their suffering. Their salty release is balm for that traumatized inner child who suffered violence for the crime of wanting to be fully seen. Like salve upon a wound, tears do not erase the pain nor eliminate scars, but they offer a chance for the body to heal itself.

What overwhelms me about this story is that these tears don't just save Jo; they actually rescue all of Israel. Jacob's twelve sons become the founders of the twelve tribes—the apocryphal forerunners of every Israelite descendant. Without the food that Jo provided, famine would have overcome the family and there would have been no twelve tribes. The survival of a people grows out of tears wept by a queer kid who endured violence—who still dared to dream of a future more radiant than their past.

It's a theme that repeats itself throughout the Bible: crying itself is not necessarily salvific, but it creates the circumstances in which God fosters new life. Perhaps the best example of this is the tears Jesus sheds over Lazarus. Recorded in the Gospel of John, the story goes that Martha and Mary send for Jesus because their brother has fallen gravely ill. "Lord, the one you love is sick," Mary writes, to which Jesus confidently replies,

"This sickness will not end in death." When he finally arrives in Judea, however, he discovers that Lazarus has already been dead and buried for four days.

Mary brings Jesus to the tomb, setting the stage for one of Christ's more famous miracles. The part of the story that has transfixed painters and preachers alike are Jesus's words at the mouth of the burial chamber: "Lazarus, come out." Upon hearing Jesus, "the dead man came out, his hands and feet wrapped with strips of linen, and a cloth around his face." It's a dramatic scene. I mean, who doesn't love a biblical mummy? But before any miracle happens, when Jesus arrives at the tomb, we get the shortest verse in all of Scripture: "Jesus wept."

Before Jesus *does* anything, he simply sits with his friends amid their sorrow. He doesn't try to fix that pain or diminish it. Nor does he keep busy or distract himself from the heartbreak that hangs leaden in the air. He is fully present and joins them in their weeping. What a gorgeous image of how we're called to show up for other people in the middle of their grief. It's a counter-cultural act that transgresses expected narratives: when people are in the throes of suffering, a sympathy card or·hot dish are certainly welcome. But a comforting, nonanxious companion in crying is worth their weight in pot roast.

When I was doing a chaplaincy internship at a hospital, my supervisor told me something I'll never forget. When we are sitting with weeping people, we often place a hand on their back and rub a small circle. Well intentioned though this may be, this gesture can communicate to the crier our own anxiety, our desire for them to stop crying, to cease doing what they're doing. Far better, she said, to simply place your hand on their back and leave it still—a gesture that says, simply, "I'm here. It's okay to cry. You're not alone."

I don't profess to fully understand Christ's miracles, but I understand his weeping. When we let our eyes run and hearts spill into that liminal space between our living and beloved dead, we resurrect those for whom we grieve in ways that transcend physical reality. Many people report that, when they are in the depths of their mourning, they feel those they've lost to be palpably nearby. Our tears seem to offer loss a blurry, corporeal form—something between a memory and a ghost. Jesus's tears prefigure Lazarus's resurrection. Knowing that he will raise Lazarus, Jesus resurrects his friend through these shared tears before he ever awakens his body.

There's beautiful symmetry, too, between the tears Jesus weeps at Lazarus's grave and those Mary Magdalene will later shed by his own. In John's Gospel, we read how she arrives at the tomb and sees the stone rolled away. She rushes to tell Simon Peter and another disciple that Jesus's body has vanished. They run to the burial place, but finding only rolled-up linen wrappings where Christ's body lay, they leave and return to their homes. Mary Magdalene stays behind, lingering in her grief. As rivers pour from her, she blinks and sees two angels, dressed in white, sitting in the tomb. They ask her why she is crying, and she responds truthfully, confessing her fear that the Romans have stolen Jesus's body. Suddenly, Jesus appears behind her and asks, "Woman, why are you weeping? Who are you looking for?" Finally, when the risen Christ calls out her name, she recognizes her friend and teacher and rushes to tell the disciples, becoming the first to proclaim his resurrection.

Again, as with Jesus and Lazarus, tears and resurrection are yoked together. The disciples flee their anguish. They are unable or unwilling—after the trauma of seeing Jesus crucified—to confront how it seems his corpse has been stolen. Mary Magdalene, however, simply lets her tears flow. She lets the harrowing grief move through her body. Through her weeping, her sorrow is transformed by the promise of new life. Again, this relationship is not incidental: the bravery to sit and hold the fullness of our hurt is what allows us to transcend it. Resurrection requires an intimacy with the death we yearn to live beyond.

This relationship between crying and transformation in sacred literature isn't confined to the Christian Scriptures, either. Other religious traditions tell similar stories about how tears change both the world and those who weep them. The Mahayana Buddhist tradition, for example, tells a story about Avalokiteshvara, the bodhisattva of compassion. It is said that Avalokiteshvara began to meditate when, all of a sudden, she confronted the vast magnitude of worldly suffering. In that moment, she was so overwhelmed she began to cry. Miraculously, those tears took a new human form: Tara, the physical embodiment of compassion. One tear became White Tara, the gentle, comforting aspect of this boundless love, while the other became Green Tara—its active, protective manifestation.

In some tellings of the story, Avalokiteshvara then saved the beings she saw in pain. However, as Zen priest Taigen Daniel Leighton describes in *Bodhisattva Archetypes*, "as she was carrying them into the Pure Land of liberation, she looked back and beheld all the spaces in samsara being filled again by new beings and her head split apart in grief." Instead of death, though, she grew two new faces from the divided halves: forever transformed by the magnitude of suffering, but given new eyes so she could see places to which she had been previously been blind. Again and again, this process repeated itself—a cycle of deliverance and suffering, until Avalokiteshvara was left with the all-seeing eleven faces with which she is often depicted.

Here, again, a common thread arises: tears may be a product of feeling distraught or even overwhelmed by worldly pain, but also they give birth to forces that both tend this hurt and seek to repair it. While in the story of Jesus and Lazarus this transpires sequentially, in the Buddhist telling it happens all at once. Avalokiteshvara's tears literally become the forces that seek to mend the harm that prompted her weeping. Gentle comfort and fierce love, held in tension, are both essential to address suffering. Eyes point in every direction, and tears now run down eleven faces that are unable to remain stoic beside worldly pain.

The prophet Muhammad similarly embodies this compassion, as recorded in the hadith, when he holds his dying son, Ibrahim. The prophet's face grows wet with tears, even trickling down into his beard, a tangible expression of Muhammad's internal sorrow. As Yahya Ibrahim of the AlMaghrib Institute describes, these tears are a sign that the prophet "experienced the revelation of the Quran as personal," not an intellectual exercise. There's something about weeping that moves us from cognitive concern toward a physical embodiment of worldly pain. Whether we're reading about Jesus or Muhammad, the message is clear: it is that movement of attention from our heads into our bodies that leads us toward the fullest expression of our humanity.

It's no coincidence that these stories about Jesus and Muhammad focus on encounters with death. The moments in which we confront the fragility of life can give us strength to live with renewed passion. On the one hand, the stories diverge: Jesus resurrects Lazarus, while Muhammad holds Ibrahim as he dies. Yet their tears are more alike than they are different. They both express the depths of their compassion for the person who has died, but they also offer an opportunity to transcend death. This is quite literal in Jesus's case. But there's something about weeping that helps free us from prisons of grief into which our loved ones' deaths might otherwise confine us. Tears affirm that we are still here. That we still love. That we will resurrect who we have lost inside ourselves as we continue living.

This interplay between tears and a chance for new life isn't just restricted to the realm of religious literature. Crying shows up again and again in secular stories at moments of personal resurrection. In Torrey Peters's novel *Detransition, Baby*, there's a particularly vivid scene in which tears lubricate a future for a character who has consigned herself to death. The novel centers on the relationship between three people: Ames, who detransitioned after living as a woman for several years; Katrina, his boss and lover, whom he has impregnated; and his exgirlfriend Reese, a trans woman who has always wanted to be a mother. Ames is uncomfortable with the idea of raising a baby with Katrina, cast in a role as father that he feels is a dysphoric simplification of his relationship to gender. So he suggests that he, Katrina, and Reese raise the child together.

Reese, while tentatively thrilled at the prospect of becoming a mother, is understandably wary about this plan, and unsure whether it stands any chance of transpiring—even after hearing that Katrina is cautiously open to the idea. It's not just pragmatic concerns Reese is wrestling with, however. Elsewhere in the book, Reese reflects openly on the ubiquity of death in trans communities, the frequency with which she attends funerals for friends and acquaintances, her fear that untimely death will be her destiny as well. Opening herself to the possibility of becoming a mother requires more than just welcoming a baby into her life. It requires she accept a different future is possible, and tears help open herself to it.

As she gets ready to meet Katrina for the first time, Reese sits down in Ames's closet, the one she used to share, and begins to weep. "She crumpled under the force of memory, her face pressed to the polyurethaned bamboo floorboards," lost somewhere between past and prophecy: "It hurt to remember hope like that." But those tears also start to erode the fatalism Reese has adopted as self-defense against a world that too often offers trans siblings far less than they deserve. In her crying, she is forced to admit that not only does she desperately long for a child; she is deserving of love.

A parallel tension manifests in "The Ark of the Turtle's Back," a short story from the indigiqueer, two-spirit speculative fiction collection *Love after the End.* Human society quivers on the brink of nonexistence. In a world of water rationing, body snatching, and off-planet forced labor, Nichiiwad is a trans woman, struggling to evade the National Indian Agency that has been pressing people to work mines on the moon. Serendipitously, she finds out through her sister that there will be a native exodus to a nearby planet perfectly suited to sustain life. Not only that, but there are doctors on this interplanetary ark who can give her a uterus. Nichiiwad is stunned: "Surgery meant womb. The technology meant I could get pregnant, have beautiful brown babies form inside me." Overcome by the prospect, Nichiiwad confesses, "This time it's my turn for the ocean to breach behind my eyes."

But suddenly she learns there's a catch: when they launch the ark from the Earth's surface, the ignition will cause the Earth to destabilize, giving it a Mars-like atmosphere, and rendering it uninhabitable. This revelation places her in an unescapable bind—forced to choose between the mother who has cradled her and her own dreams of delivering life into the universe. Eventually, she chooses the possibility of new life, even though abandoning Earth feels like sacrificing beloved family. Indeed, Nichiiwad seems to viscerally experience the planet's fate as "sobs ripple through [her] shoulders like earthquakes . . . a dry wail billowing out of [her] throat like ribbon in a prairie tornado."

Whereas Reese weeps because the prospect of shared parenthood forces her to confront the ways she'd tacitly expected to die, Nichiiwad cries because she is now able to bring life into a world that's dying. Tears feel curiously at home in this utopian story, set in a distressingly familiar dystopia. Crying is a way to resist the lure of futility without denying the underlying truths that make numbness so seductive. It freely admits we are enmeshed in a disintegrating social fabric, but refuses to concede that these tattered remains are the only materials we possess to weave a future. In both, crying is an inextricable part of a broader transformation. Crying allows characters to open themselves to new worlds even as they mourn what they are losing.

I'm fascinated by tears in utopian fiction because their very existence beautifully violates the false pretense that paradise would be a place where tears never flow. There's a verse in the book of Revelation that I long struggled with: a promise that in the new earth, God "will wipe every tear from their eyes" (Revelation 21:4). I used to read that as a promise that God's future would be a world without weeping, until someone pointed out that they read that passage simply as a promise that every tear would be held. For who's to say God doesn't collect those tears rather than dispose of them? Utopian fiction doesn't pretend that all our problems must be solved before birthing something new. Paradise is what we build in the middle of this mess. Tears lubricate that journey: aligning us with our true desires, helping us relinquish narratives that no longer serve us, and cultivating courage to pursue new life amid the ruins of old pain.

The inverse of how tears function in utopian fiction is a kind of weeping that can launch people toward villainy. Just as surely as Alice's tears opened a portal to wonder, tears can open up bitter, tragic dimensions. Sometimes pain isn't transformed into personal growth. Sometimes trauma becomes twisted with hatred, distorting people into gaunt and haunted shadows.

"La Llorona" is a Mexican folktale that embodies just how deep grief can plunge us. Literally translated as "The Crying One," the story about a weeping woman goes as far back as the Aztec empire or earlier. As in any folktale, the details vary somewhat from telling to telling, but the core description remains the same: La Llorona is a ghostly figure who wails into the night, mourning the children she has killed. During her life, she had devolved into madness after her husband left her for another woman. Having discovered his deception and in tremendous grief, she murdered her children. In many renditions of the story, she drowns them and then herself—the family quite literally consumed by a lake or river of tears.

If your high school reading list was anything like mine, you might notice strong parallels between La Llorona and Medea of Greek myth, who kills her sons after Jason leaves her to marry Glauke. (Evidently, shitty men are very much a cross-cultural phenomenon.) In Euripides's story, too, Medea weeps copiously after learning of the betrayal and as she ponders the unfathomable decision to murder their children. As she cries, Jason asks her, "Medea, why weep and fill your eyes with these pale tears?" Real catch, Jason. Indeed Jason's remarkable insensitivity is apparently what finally pushes her over the edge. "It's nothing," she answers ominously. "I was thinking of the children."

In these stories, the act of crying brings the mothers into stark confrontation with the harm they've suffered. Weeping strips away any comforting lies, rejects their partners' attempts to placate the damage they've left in their wake. All that's left is the enormity of pain, and the desire to make her husband feel the depths of her own suffering. Tears mark both the resolution to murder their children and the consequences of that choice. With a conscience so thoroughly drowned, the protagonist becomes a monster.

If these stories show how weeping can yield monstrosity, the epic poem *Beowulf* shows how even monsters are not immune from weeping. Beowulf is a legendary warrior—the epitome of medieval heroic masculinity—who embarks on a quest to Heorot, the majestic hall of the king Hrothgar. Every night for decades a fearsome creature, Grendel, has descended upon the palace to murder its inhabitants. This reign of terror meets an abrupt end, however, when Beowulf tears Grendel's arm from his body, sending him howling into the Danish night.

But this battle is just the opening act. Grendel, in his dying moments, runs home to his mom and dies in her arms. Grendel's mother, mad with grief, swears vengeance on Hrothgar and Heorot, setting up the ultimate confrontation between Beowulf and Grendel's mother. In her fabulous new translation of the text, Maria Dhavana Headley points out that Grendel's mother "is almost always depicted in translation as an obvious monster rather than a human woman," even though the Old English lends itself to either choice. It's less morally complex to simply write her off as a beast, even though, according to Headley, "Grendel's mother doesn't behave like a monster. She behaves like a bereaved mother who happens to have a warrior's skill." It's much more comfortable to dismiss her as a mythical hag or ogress than to face the depths of harm to which pain can drive us.

Medievalist Jeffrey Cohen points out that monsters always lurk at the doorway of unspoken fears. They serve as embodied gatekeepers policing the borders of human behavior—dire threats of the fate awaiting anyone who transgresses these social boundaries. "They can be pushed to the farthest margins of geography and discourse, hidden away at the edges of the world and in the forbidden recesses of our mind, but they always return," Cohen writes. "They ask us why we have created them." *Beowulf* doesn't just celebrate peace through masculine violence; it warns against the danger of women consumed by grief, tears that can render them inhuman.

I wonder if, without weeping, La Llorona or Medea simply recede into emptiness. Had they transmuted that pain into deadened numbness, would they have slain their kids? Likewise, if Grendel's mother had suppressed her tears, would she have sought vengeance at Heorot? No doubt, from a moral perspective, most people consider that preferable, and ethicists would agree. Yet as a reader, I can't help but feel that I don't want to live in a world where men leave brokenness in their wake and women are left to quietly sit within it. I'm not defending their actions, but somehow the stories without their vengeance seem even less tolerable.

Again we find a stubborn link between tears and transformation, even amid these harrowing circumstances. These women are transformed into something terrible, yes. But it is undeniable that they are forever changed by these episodes of weeping. While hopefully we can employ somewhat more adaptive coping mechanisms than these mythic protagonists, the moral of these tales cannot be that the crying, itself, was wrong. Without it, we are barely human. The absence of feeling is what's truly monstrous.

Charles Dickens's *A Christmas Carol* opens with a man perched upon the precipice of losing what's left of his humanity. Ebenezer Scrooge does not cry; Dickens is quite clear about this. Even upon the death of his partner and only friend, Jacob Marley, Scrooge was "not so dreadfully cut up by the sad event," choosing to commemorate his passing by striking a bargain on the coffin. "Hard and sharp as flint, from which no steel had ever struck out generous fire," is how Dickens describes him; "the cold within him froze his old features" so thoroughly that any tear would be crystal long before it left his ducts. This isn't just a story about a frigid miser learning to love Christmas and develop a penchant for generosity. It's a tale of someone learning how to feel.

Time and again, Scrooge is moved to tears as the ghosts usher him through past, present, and future. When he sees himself "as a lonely boy reading near a feeble fire," we read how Scrooge "wept to see his poor forgotten self as he used to be." Forced to confront the striking solitude that shaped him, the image "fell upon the heart of Scrooge with a softening influence, and gave a freer passage to his tears." When the Spirit of Christmas Present tells Scrooge that Tiny Tim will die, leaving "a crutch without an owner, carefully preserved," Scrooge becomes distraught, "overcome with penitence and grief." By the time that the Ghost of Christmas Yet to Come shows Scrooge his own corpse lying in a casket, this man who once bargained on his friend's is pleading, "let me see some tenderness connected with a death."

When Scrooge finally awakes from these visions, crying is the visible sign of his rebirth: "He had been sobbing violently with the Spirit, and his face was wet with tears." With his body feeling "light as a feather . . . giddy as a drunken man," he begins to make extravagant plans to transform his life—raining bounty on the Cratchit family, making Christmas plans with his spurned nephew, "laughing and crying in the same breath." Once again, we see that tears are not just the *product* of a conversion. The act of crying—of reacquainting himself with his emotions—is what thaws Scrooge's heart and makes that dramatic metamorphosis possible.

You could write an entire book about the different ways that crying shows up in literature, and any brief survey like this threatens to flatten that diversity. And there's clearly an inherent artificiality in generalizing about the ways tears shape characters in fiction or myth or sacred texts; the authors, after all, chose to include weeping at particular points in the narrative to heighten tension, emphasize emotional response, or provide an outward manifestation of internal change. But what makes great literature, myth, and scripture powerful is their honest resonance. Things don't happen in the real world exactly as the authors describe, yet there is an undeniable spark within the story that makes our own hearts leap in recognition. When the same pattern emerges in genres as widely divergent as sacred literature, Afrofuturism, trans realism, indigiqueer speculative fiction, Greek myth, and Mexican folklore, it's a good indication that these tropes align with deeper truth.

Tears and transformation are intrinsically yoked in literature and in life. Crying is a liminal space where we can confront what we truly desire, what we're grieving, what we fear. It's a portal to the parts of us that we've repressed or shut away. You simply can't lie to yourself when you're wracked by sobs. Like Alice, crying brings us to the threshold of new and frightening revelation: we may not like what we see, but there is a decided comfort in knowing ourselves better and risking to follow where our weeping leads.

This relationship builds on the ways crying knits us in community. No one transforms wholly by ourselves—all change happens within our broader relationships. Indeed, an important predictor of what *kind* of transformation we undergo is the degree to which we're connected to people who support and nurture growth. One reason Grendel's mother or Medea or La Llorona become monsters may be the punishing isolation in which their grief curdles. As we saw in the previous chapter, crying signals to the people around us that we need support, and makes them more likely to offer it. And it creates space for us to psychologically process pain, while simultaneously offering catharsis. No wonder authors have, for millennia, linked tears to metamorphosis. Tears both open a door and help us walk through it.

So if crying is a fundamental human act—essential for our psychological and social health, and a potent opportunity for transformation—why don't we cry more frequently? How have we built a culture where some folks stop crying altogether?

CHAPTER 4

Cowboys Don't Cry

McKinley Sims grew up in the West Texas panhandle. Raised on cattle ranches by his grandfather, McKinley remembers his granddad's favorite adage: "Cowboys don't cry." Sims and I are roughly the same age, but our early years were strikingly different. "The only acceptable masculine emotion was anger," Sims recalls. "Any kind of tenderness, any outward display of emotion, was culturally frowned upon."

Paul David Benedict, who grew up in the Seattle suburbs, was an emotional child, quick to cry. That all changed when his family moved to rural Iowa, to a place that required a seventy-mile trip to the nearest McDonald's. In this new town, all the grades were grouped together in school, and Benedict soon became the target of older kids for whom tears did not fit the accepted masculine ideal. "I was called a girl," he remembers. "I was called gay a lot—even though I don't think the kids even knew what that meant. It was just the thing to throw at somebody who presents as weak. I'd be made fun of for crying. It becomes a vicious cycle where you try to bury those things, but it just becomes more debilitating."

Tim Tutt was four years old when his grandfather died, and on the day of the funeral, his mother was helping him get dressed in a smart suit for little boys: white jacket and shorts, patent leather shoes and knee socks. He recalls her plain instruction as she helped him with the bowtie: "Your grandmother may cry, and I may cry, but whatever you do: do not cry." Her hands twisted and jerked the tie to emphasize the words, and they became a mantra Tutt never forgot.

Mohammad Mia says that when he was growing up, "the message I received was that crying is something private and shameful—something that you do by yourself when you feel overwhelmed but not something you share or let other people know that you've done." Now he sees that this environment was in large part a product of the trauma his parents carried. "They didn't know that people would have your back if you expressed any weakness," he notes. "It made it hard for them to have emotional language, to share it with other people, and to know that they can be safe and held in that vulnerability."

In talking about the tear-deprived, it's only fitting to begin with men. Men are not the only people whose weeping is stigmatized, and the next chapters will explore particular challenges other folks encounter. But it's important to start with men for two reasons. First: study after study has confirmed that men cry significantly less frequently than women and gender-inventive folks. In fact, the first research to compare tears across gender found that the most common number of crying episodes in a month for male participants was zero. Clearly, something sturdy and deeply embedded is blocking our ability to weep.

Teasing apart nature and nurture when parsing psychological phenomena is usually tricky. But tearlessness is clearly an example of social forces overwhelming our innate biological predisposition. As we saw in the previous chapter, crying is healthy, even essential for both our psychological and physiological well-being.

It developed in humans because it's evolutionarily adaptive, and it is quite clearly a feature of normal child development. The phenomenon of dry-eyed men is far too pervasive to be explained on a case-by-case basis. Widespread social problems demand systemic explanations.

Male discomfort with grief—particularly white male aversion to it—also plays a significant role in other folks' barriers to weeping. We will look in this chapter at how that happens. A full autopsy of what has broken men is integral to understanding what is breaking our siblings.

So what is robbing men of our full emotional expression? And what happens to all the tears men leave uncried?

There's a scene in the holiday classic *A Christmas Story* in which the protagonist, nine-year-old Ralphie Parker, is walking by himself when, from nowhere, he's hit in the face by a snowball. He turns and sees the town bully, Skut Farcas, and his sidekick cackling. Instinctively, Ralphie's eyes begin to well up. Sensing the imminent tears, Farcas leaps from the car where he's sitting. "What, are you gonna cry?" he sneers. "C'mon crybaby, cry for me! C'mon, cry!"

Suddenly the tears that were forming beneath his lids retreat, and the narrator begins to speak: "Deep in the recesses of my brain, a tiny red-hot flame began to grow." Ralphie's quivering lip turns instead to a grimace, and he launches himself at Farcas, swearing and pummeling his face. His sorrow-turned-rage is interrupted only by the arrival of his mother, who tears him away, leaving Farcas bloodied and wailing on the ground.

These two minutes paint such a vivid picture of the emotional transformation that afflicts many men. It begins with Ralphie on the verge of crying, which is the normal, healthy reaction to the physical pain of hurled ice and the emotional anguish of taunts and jeers. But ultimately, being shamed for crying has more longstanding consequences than any snowball's sting. Note the form those stifled tears take: clenched fists and frenzied blows. So often anger covers our deepest hurt. An easy way to keep from crying is to force your own tears onto someone else.

Obviously, not all admonitions against crying come in the form of a racoon-skin-capped bully screaming "C'mon crybaby, cry for me!" (Though frankly, the scene's pathos stems from how ordinary it is to demonize tears.) But if it were only the occasional cartoon villain, most men would probably have an easier time resisting a cultural demand for stoicism. It's much harder when that message is communicated in a thousand, subtler ways.

I was blessed to grow up in a family who never told me not to cry. While my own father didn't weep often, he didn't hide it when he did, and he and my mother expressly told me to embrace my emotions. When I did cry—which was fairly often in those days— they never told me to stop. They'd sit with me and offer comfort. I never got the impression that my tears were a burden, and they certainly never shamed me for them.

But like all children do, I was growing up in a culture larger than the one my parents could create at home. And like most boys' childhoods are, mine was filled with interactions that vilified weeping. I remember playing soccer at recess in second grade. Lord knows I can't recall the score, or even what happened, but we lost and a boy on our team began to cry. Showing that knack for childhood cruelty, some boys on the opposing team, and several on ours, began to taunt him. Relentlessly. Of course, this only made the situation worse: his crying intensified, launching an awful feedback loop only broken when some wise teacher caught on to what was happening and intervened. I don't remember if I joined in the jeers—though knowing my insecurities at the time, I probably did—but I do know that I made a mental note: crying was *definitely* not something to do among one's peers.

I didn't yet stop crying altogether, but I learned to sequester my tears into private moments. If I became incredibly frustrated, I'd let it emerge as anger, saving softness for my bedroom. If stung by a classmate's verbal barb, I'd return an insult in kind, hiding how much it hurt me. This pattern—burying tears any time they threatened to emerge—repeated itself until it was no longer conscious. Tamping down one's emotions is a skill that, like any other, becomes instinctive and habitual. By the time I finished elementary school, I can't remember a time when I cried around other people. Crying isn't usually extinguished by some traumatic incident but rather by long attrition from a world that refuses to carve out space for it. As bell hooks so aptly put it, "The first act of violence that patriarchy demands of males is not violence toward women. Instead, patriarchy demands of all males that they engage in acts of psychic self-mutilation, that they kill off the emotional parts of themselves."

Once, when I was working in retail, a woman and her husband came into the store with their toddler son to pick out shoes. Instantly the boy became infatuated with a pair of pink sneakers. I asked them what size shoe he wore so he could try them on, and the father became enraged. "No son of mine is going to wear pink shoes!" he shouted. Instantly, his child's cherubic little face crumpled, and he burst into tears. The wails just further enraged the father, who shoved a pair of gray sneakers onto his boy's feet, marched him to the register, and bought them while he howled.

This is just a small example of traditional male paradigms being forced on boys, but its banality for me is very much the point. A child thrilled at the prospect of wearing bright, colorful shoes instead learned a harsh lesson about what his father's approval requires, and about how weeping will be punished.

Shoving tears deeper and deeper into the recesses of your life has a striking effect on your ability to produce them. When men train their bodies, even for a minute, to deny tears when they arise, they create an emotional and spiritual barrier between their experience of emotion and its release. It's why, now, I try very hard never to hold back tears. Numbness isn't something I ever wish to cultivate again. Granting your body immediate release reinforces those emotional pathways suppression has deadened.

When men cry openly, it also normalizes crying as a social activity. When young boys learn to wait until they are by themselves, it alienates them from whatever grief, frustration, and hurt they may be carrying. When we cry around other emotionally healthy people, they ask us, "What's wrong?" or offer comfort. It contextualizes crying within a broader community that loves and supports you. Conversely, isolation creates the illusion that tears are shameful, something to be relegated from public view, like shoplifting or eating an entire carton of Peeps.

As I spoke to more and more men about what they learned about tears, the same themes popped up repeatedly. The lessons likely won't surprise you. "Out on the football field, if you got knocked down, if it hurt, you couldn't cry about it," McKinley Sims remembers. Sims's childhood on a Texas ranch strikes me as a life that I, as a bookish, weepy kid, might have seen on television. But whereas I had channeled my growing boyhood aversion to tears into numbness, he was taught to express it through aggression: "Be tough. Shake it off. Get back up. Hit them harder."

Sims tells me that when he was young, he was often responsible for opening heavy cattle gates so his grandfather could drive the truck through them. The latches were heavy and required a lot of strength to budge, which made it a difficult task for a child. He recalls getting so frustrated trying to open them that it would bring him to the brink of tears—only to have his granddad again tell him, "Hey now, cowboys don't cry."

Being told that your natural, innate response is not acceptable cuts deeply. "Shame would set in," Sims remembers. "Not only was I doing something wrong in the physical world—I couldn't perform this action correctly—but I was also just not the right kind of person. So it wasn't just about doing something wrong but being something wrong as well."

When he says those words to me over the phone, it's as if something clicks inside me. I may not have had any experience opening and shutting heavy ranch gates, but that feeling of not just doing something wrong but *being* something wrong? That I know all too intimately. Toxic masculinity is far from an exclusive export of the Texas Panhandle. The message may manifest in different guises, but that feeling of incorrect embodiment holds steady.

The tipping point for Paul David Benedict, whose family moved to rural Iowa, where he was ridiculed by older children in his small school, came as he finally sought help. "I was crying in front of the teacher, within eyeshot of the rest of the class," Benedict says. "I was used to teachers being protector figures, places to go to when I was in distress. But I just remember the look of utter confusion, even horror on his face—essentially, 'Why is this boy crying in front of me?'"

The teacher's lack of response was not the only epiphany for Benedict. "I remember looking around at the class and seeing their confusion and disapproval," he says. "It was almost the confusion that hurt more than the disapproval. Suddenly I realized: It's not safe. These emotions, whatever experience I'm having—it's just not safe to have that externally. I remember trying hard after that to not process those emotions externally. I think that stunted my ability to process them internally."

For Benedict, this manifested as social anxiety—a feeling that he couldn't be vulnerable or authentic around others. He developed the ability to present a tough exterior even though it didn't match his own internal life. Suffering stranded him in the gap between his true identity and the version of himself he felt the world wanted to see.

When Tim Tutt's mother told him not to cry at his grandfather's funeral, he says, "I took that story into my body. I said to myself, 'Boys don't cry.' I don't know that I really cried again out of true emotion until my other grandfather died when I was thirty. So from the time I was four until I was thirty, I don't remember crying in any kind of emotional way."

What's fascinating is that, whereas Sims received old-fashioned Texan anger as a substitute and Benedict retreated behind a false exterior, Tutt learned to charm and perform. "I remember walking into the funeral, down the center aisle of the church in the family procession," he says, "and I remember friends of my grandmother's seated in the congregation, and as we walked by my grandmother's friend turned to her neighbor and said in a very loud whisper, 'Oh he's just precious, he's such an angel.'" Tutt remembers being filled with pride at the compliment. Looking back now, he sees how performing became an internalized strategy for navigating pain. The lesson was that "being cute is how you really make your way through the world, rather than being vulnerable or emotional," he concludes. "I learned in that moment that if I presented well in public, if I had a nice facade, then that's what the world wanted from me more than true vulnerability."

Although these three men learned this lesson in markedly different contexts, and all coped in different ways, there's a tragic similarity in the effects of suppressing tears. All three express deep regret for the years during which an authentic emotional life was stolen from them. All speak of the lingering difficulty it takes to overcome that tragic inheritance. "Before, I had this shame and guilt from crying," Sims recalls. "But then as I got older and realized 'Oh, this is the wrong way,' then I had shame in the other direction: that I'm not emotionally accessible. So it's been a journey of reclaiming wholeness. If you're shutting down part of yourself, then you're not really whole."

It's tempting to blithely ascribe this rejection of tears to toxic masculinity, roll our eyes, and move on. Tearlessness is merely one more symptom of an inclination toward aggression and violence. Not much new there.

But I think the truth is much more revealing. The way men learn to extinguish our own tears even before they fall is a principal *cause* of toxic masculine behavior, not only its result. Crying is often an outgrowth of empathy—a physical manifestation of our ability to connect deeply to others' emotional states, to feel them reflected in our own. To effectively curtail the human tendency to weep, we must sever the connections that tether our spirit to our neighbor's. This vicious cycle, between internal repression and external harm, is one we must interrupt.

Patriarchal abuse, in its myriad forms, is an expression of power. The ability to inflict violence on another while maintaining positive self-regard isn't just a product of dehumanizing the victim of that aggression. Nor is it solely driven by the desire to exert control and dominance over someone else. It is also grounded in the power to control one's own emotional states, to lock away our natural and healthy proclivity to share each other's pain. We learn this skill by first practicing on ourselves, dismissing the pain *we* experience as unworthy of regard, care, or attention.

This isn't to excuse men who commit acts of violence or to say they're just victims of a culture that has stunted their ability to feel. Any abuse is monstrous. But in the true etymological sense of monster—from the Latin *monstrare*, "a sign or omen that reveals a deeper truth"—men who abuse others are acting out and underscoring a quotidian violence. Their behavior discloses more than they know.

This lasting damage is readily apparent in the reactions to prominent men—particularly those in positions of power and leadership—who break this culturally expected tearlessness.

In January 2017, President Donald Trump banned refugees from Muslim-majority countries from entering the US. Soon after the ban was announced, Senator Chuck Schumer stood beside a dozen new Americans and gave an emotional address. Citing the words of Emma Lazarus—"Give me your tired, your poor, your huddled masses yearning to breathe free"—Schumer then took a breath. "This executive order was mean-spirited and un-American," he concluded, eyes brimming.

Those tears should not be remarkable. The leader of our country had just signed a deeply bigoted directive, endangering the safety of hundreds of thousands of refugees and immigrants and effectively cutting off millions more from their friends and family. Nor was Schumer's speech particularly radical. "Mean-spirited" is about the nicest thing you can call executive brutality, and while calling the action "un-American" may be ahistorical, it's hardly offensive. And it's not as if he broke down sobbing at the podium; the most we saw was a saline glimmer behind Schumer's glasses. Yet many Americans became enraged at the sight of the Senator's unshed tears.

"We all saw Minority Leader Chuck Schumer well up in croco-dile tears as he derided the president's perfectly legal and highly prudent executive order," wrote Fox News commentator Sean Hannity. "I don't recall Schumer crying after the terror attacks in San Bernardino." Senator David Perdue declared, "The Mi-nority Leader's 'tear-jerking' performance over the past weekend belonged at the Screen Actors Guild Awards, not in a serious dis-cussion of what it takes to keep America safe"—as if compassion was incompatible with safety.

Predictably, President Trump himself joined the mocking chorus. In an interview response, he said "I saw Chuck Schumer with fake tears. I'm gonna ask him who is his acting coach." It became such a defining moment in the Fox News extended uni-verse that, years later, Trump would still regularly refer to the senator as "Cryin' Chuck Schumer."

Trump's chronic and disturbing dearth of empathy is not news. Yet transcending his own pathology was the indisputable fact that his petty barbs found widespread purchase among a gleeful public. Trump is awful at many things—diplomacy, moral imagination, decorating—but one of his genuine talents is an ability to shrewdly read a room. "Cryin' Chuck Schumer" caught on because it draws from that deep well of masculine sickness that perceives any vulnerability as weakness.

While ridiculing the notion that someone might care for refugees is a symptom of that deep national illness, it also highlights the brittleness and fragility of toxic masculinity. Men attack other men who cry because, at some level, they sense their own emotional deficiencies. The tears in another's eyes renders them painfully aware of the dusty, barren husks of their own sockets. And it's why, in the end, men's open weeping will always carry power.

When President Obama took the podium on December 14, 2012, after the massacre at Sandy Hook, he could have made a fiery speech. He could have howled about the evil of a gun lobby that makes firearms easier and easier to acquire, and about the way that legislators chose fealty to gun manufacturers over the lives of children. That anger would have been righteous.

Instead, Obama spoke softly into the microphone and cried. "The majority of those who died today were children, beautiful little kids between the ages of five and ten years old," he said. "They had their entire lives ahead of them: birthdays, graduations, kids of their own." As he spoke, he wiped the tears that trickled down his cheek—not drawing attention to them, but not doing anything to hide them either.

What else can you do when children are slaughtered? In that moment, emotional integrity is our deepest strength. Those children deserved a nation awash in tears, and they deserved a president honest about his own sorrow. And it's the kind of pain that lingers. Four years later, when calling for comprehensive gun reform, President Obama again spoke with tears streaming down his cheeks. "Our inalienable right to life, liberty and the pursuit of happiness," he began, "those rights were stripped . . . from first graders in Newtown. First graders." But then he stopped speaking altogether, letting his tears speak a lament our mouths alone never can. "Every time I think about those kids, I get mad," he said. But he didn't look angry. He looked heartbroken, and his words resonated with a nation whose hearts were breaking as well.

Conservative pundits tried to portray his weeping as disingenuous. But that's one of the striking things about crying: in those moments when tears are the only human reaction, mockery only underscores a bully's inhumanity. "It's really not believable," said Fox News host Andrea Tantaros. Ben Shapiro tweeted a GIF of James Van Der Beek's overwrought sobs on *Dawson's Creek*. But what was truly unbelievable was not that a president cried; it was how people could look on this unending slaughter with dry eyes.

Set against cultural expectations that demand we gaze upon even murdered children without becoming emotional, men's tears hold formidable power. The crying man is immediately rendered different, set apart by his emotional honesty. And because of the way men wield power, the presence of those tears grants tacit permission to everyone else to cry as well.

Clearly, people should not need to wait for men to catch up emotionally for their own tears to become socially acceptable. This is another function of patriarchy. Yet as long as we live in a culture where men hold outsized influence, weeping men can actively subvert it. Indeed, the Ben Shapiros of the world fear crying men because they understand—correctly—the threat men's tears pose to patriarchal structures. In order to justify their role as inherent provider and protector, men have to resist any behavior that suggests vulnerability or weakness. After all, if men aren't somehow physiologically superior—better able to emotionally endure suffering and hardship—why should we deserve better pay, cultural autonomy, and the right to control the women and children in our lives?

When men weep, it highlights the central lie propping up this façade: men aren't physiologically distinct. We're not inherently "less emotional" or "more objective." Given a healthy socialization and upbringing, we too tear up in hard times and sob amid tragedy. When men cry, the supposed "strength" of a brittle and unfeeling disposition is revealed to be pathology. Tearless, emotionally stunted men are set in stark contrast to men who have recovered the ability to fully feel—or who never lost that power in the first place.

It's a power that explains why Fred Rogers left such an indelible imprint on my own life and the lives of so many children who grew up watching him. Mr. Rogers's neighborhood created a liminal space where emotions—particularly sad and painful ones—were named and held. The words of one of his most famous songs speak directly to a child in anguish: "What do you do with the mad that you feel, when you feel so mad you could bite? When the whole wide world feels oh so wrong, and nothing you do feels very right?" Mr. Rogers knew that anger and frustration so often cover the deep sorrow children and adults experience. It's much easier to paper over that pain with rage. But hopping that trolley toward emotional honesty provides a path between anger and despondency.

Speaking to Congress in defense of public television, Mr. Rogers made clear this gift was intentional. "If we in public television can only make it clear that feelings are mentionable and manageable, we will have done a great service for mental health," he said. "I think it's much more dramatic to show that two men could be working out their feelings of anger than showing something of gunfire. I'm constantly concerned by what our children are seeing. . . . I've been trying to show a meaningful expression of care."

That care didn't just speak *to* children; it modeled a tenderness that stared unblinkingly at pain and responded with fragile love. In one episode, Mr. Rogers talks about the death of his child-hood dog, Mitsy. "I was very sad when she died," he says, "because she and I were good pals. And when she died, I cried. . . . I really missed her." That kind of emotional modeling from men in a child's life deliberately subverts the power of anger or stoicism that's too frequently portrayed as strength.

But Mr. Rogers didn't just speak about the pain brought by external tragedy; he also specifically named the existential feelings of inadequacy that can also prompt our tears. Singing through Daniel Tiger, he conjectured, "Sometimes I wonder if I'm a mistake. I'm not supposed to be scared, am I? Sometimes I cry, and sometimes I shake, wondering 'isn't it true that the strong never break?'" Talking openly about our tears and our own insecurities limits other people's power to wield them as a club. If this were normative for every child, I have no doubt fewer men would pick up actual weapons.

In his final appearance on his television show, Fred Rogers offered words I still turn to amid my own tears. "I know how tough it is some days to look with hope and confidence on the months and years ahead," he said. "But I would like to tell you what I often told you when you were much younger: 'I like you just the way you are.'"

What a gift to children: I like you in your tears, in your pain, in everything that makes you *you*. You don't need to pretend to be strong when you feel weak, or glad when you feel sad. You can simply be, and know that it will always be enough.

Mr. Rogers's openhearted masculinity is enjoying a bit of a renais-sance. Beyond an award-winning documentary *Won't You Be My*

Neighbor and Tom Hanks's portrayal in *A Beautiful Day in the Neighborhood*, Mr. Rogers's gentleness is being reincarnated in a variety of popular culture outlets. Contemporary entertainers and social media accounts have embraced the overwhelming hunger for kind, empathic, and even weepy men.

Nick Cho operates the hugely popular TikTok account YourKoreanDad, where he speaks directly to you as the viewer, as if you were his child. An average episode might depict Nick sitting across the table at a restaurant, or eating a particularly delicious piece of fruit. But throughout, his deep care and concern—and his willingness to honor the pain so many carry on the other side of the screen—has attracted more than three million followers.

It's no coincidence that this rise to stardom coincided with the devastation of a global pandemic. When so many people felt alone and isolated, the bluster of men who pretended we could bloviate our way through millions of deaths rang sickeningly hollow. Rather than dismiss our fears or sadnesses, Cho names them directly. "I see a lot of you heartbroken," he says in one video, "and for some of you, it's just letting something out. And to all of that, I just want to say, 'I'm so proud of you.' It's a good thing to show your emotions. It's a good thing to share that with others."

As I weep on my side of the digital feed, it's not just a video anymore; it's an authentic, emotional connection Cho is forming with millions. What we're feeling is good and right, he says; in fact, it's the very best of what makes us human.

Watching one of his videos, I decided to reach out to Cho to see if he'd have time for a conversation, and he agreed. As we talked via Zoom, it became clear that while YourKoreanDad is a character Cho plays, the care and intention that fills his videos is abundantly real. He's a dad in real life, too, and old artwork by his kids dots the wall behind him. His demeanor is lighthearted, but when he talks about his project, it's clear how much love he devotes to a single minute-long video. "I'm always looking for some unmet need and desire that I might be able to speak to," he says. "There's an intimate space between the TikTok screen and people, especially young people, very often curled up in bed for hours. For me it was like, 'What do I have to offer that deserves to be in that intimate space?'"

While YourKoreanDad is a relatively new project, it's also an extension of his lifelong commitment to making people feel seen and valued. "I thought I was going to be a pastor when I was nineteen or twenty years old," he tells me, a bit sheepishly. "But I realized I wasn't meant to be an ordained minister." Now, however, Cho's videos succeed where many pulpits fail. And he articulates an interconnectedness often missing in religious spaces. "The interesting thing about a dad," he says, "is that a dad is not singular. There's no such thing as a dad on an island by themselves. A dad is subordinate to someone: the implied kid. So in a way, I'm actually submitting myself to the viewer and making them the main character."

And it's clear from the reaction to his videos just how many people are hungry for a masculine presence that makes them feel cared for and centered—someone who makes *them* the main character in their own story. "People crying when they were watching my content was very confusing at first," he admits. "There was a video of me going to Walgreens like, 'Let's get some snacks,' that received dozens of videos of people crying. And their captions asked, 'Is this what it's like to have a dad? Is this what a dad is supposed to be like? My dad isn't like that.'"

The responses to that simple video surprised him. "People have been so abused and neglected by the men in their lives," he says. "You can only imagine the fan mail I get. It's very heavy, and some of it completely ruins me. A lot of it has made *me* cry." But in this reciprocal exchange, Cho plants the seeds for new kinds of masculinity to flourish, ones that aren't confined to the sins of our past.

Many men find it easier to cry about someone else than to weep for themselves. This, too, is a function of power, and the ways that men are socialized to wield it. If I cry for my wife, my tears are still neatly aligned with my socially expected role as protector and provider. Though obviously a welcome deviation from the strictest stoic masculinity, those tears still place me as the solid bedrock upon which others may find rest. But it doesn't necessarily mean that I'm willing to own my own pain and vulnerability.

It's into this emotional ambivalence that Ted Lasso confidently strides. The television show *Ted Lasso* burst onto the streaming television scene as a cult passion, warming countless hearts with its wholesome titular protagonist. Ted is an American football coach hired to helm an English Premier League football team. Though he knows nothing about soccer, Lasso quickly wins over the English public—and the viewer—with his relentless optimism and gentle leadership. Accustomed to the fiery antics of Bobby Knight or Coach K, audiences find Jason Sudeikis's character willfully subverting these tropes. Lasso is a coach who, in the third episode, proudly proclaims to a reporter that he doesn't care whether the team wins or loses so long as they do it together.

We're so used to leaders who berate players when they make a mistake that this gentleness is startlingly effective. (I once had a coach who would reach down to the floor of the gym and mime picking up the testicles you'd left behind. It doesn't take the Buddha himself to be a welcome deviation from *that* norm.) When one player makes a glaring error in practice, Ted Lasso advises him to "be a goldfish" and immediately forget it. When his star striker repeatedly reveals himself to be more interested in being a prat than a teammate, Ted relies on relentless kindness to win him over.

All the while, however, there's a stark disconnect between the love Coach Lasso offers his players and what he directs inward. Ted's marriage ends during the first season, and while he routinely engages in deep conversation with everyone from the team owner to the equipment manager, he seems unable to let people see the pain he's going through. The only scenes in which this sorrow breaks through are ones in which he's literally alone in the dark—at a hotel room, in his office, or by himself in bed. He continues to maintain a relentlessly optimistic veneer—nothing but tender support for everyone in his life, including even his wife when she lets him know she just doesn't love him anymore. But behind that caring grin, his own mental health is crumbling.

This chasm continues to widen until it reaches its breaking point: in the middle of a match, Ted dramatically leaves the pitch, gripped by a panic attack. No one can find him when the game ends, and he is uncharacteristically absent from the team's victory celebration. Finally, the team psychologist returns to her office to find Coach Lasso crying, shrouded in the dark and very much alone.

The remainder of the second season centers on Ted finally learning to process the emotions he has neglected for so long. He cries again when he finally lets his mask slip: he reveals to Dr. Sharon that he came home and found his father on the day he killed himself. He confesses the rage he still feels for his dad, and the brokenness he left behind. Finally, he begins to bawl when Dr. Sharon asks him what he loved about his dad. "He was a good dad," Lasso admits, "and I don't think he knew that. I think if he would have known how good he was at stuff he didn't really care about being good at, I don't think he would have done what he did. And I wish I would have told him more."

The tears aren't the end of Ted's healing journey; they are more an invitation to begin. At the end of the season Dr. Sharon leaves, and Ted is left with the glaring truth: if he's going to become emotionally healthy, he may benefit from guidance. But ultimately, some parts of this work he must do for himself.

American masculinity is very much in a Ted Lasso moment, caught somewhere between the toxicity of John Wayne and the tenderness of Mr. Rogers. Many millennial and Gen Z men were raised with or have developed an openness and vulnerability that dwarfs the male socialization of past generations. And yet that poisoned air still lingers. Many regard tears with ambivalence. Others are intellectually convinced they are healthy but unable to comfortably cry.

And then there's what writer Daniel José Camacho sees as a kind of "performative tenderness" among men, particularly in online spaces. "I think that with social media, because of the algorithms and what gets the most attention," he says, "there's a pressure to perform a kind of vulnerability, and there's so much out there that I think is bullshit—it's not real vulnerability."

Given that I'm something of a vulnerability evangelist and that I spend far too much time online talking about my feels, I'm surprised by how readily I agree with him. There has been a definite tilt toward effusive and expansive emotional expression in spaces like Twitter. But I don't know that this vulnerability is fully reflective of how people are changing in their own lives. It's like men are inching closer to fuller emotional expression but doing it on our own terms, at safe remove from actual humans. After all, it's much easier to type tender things from the psychological remove of a keyboard than to say them when looking someone in the eyes (or staring at yourself in a mirror). "Being vulnerable with someone is being intimate with someone," Camacho deftly articulates, and there's a gap between the vulnerability we're expressing and the intimacy we're cultivating. The portrayal of softness can be a shortcut around the harder work of becoming soft. Tears are such a crucial part of narrowing that gap.

The good news is that men recognizing the harm of suppressing their tears isn't just a fictional trope confined to TikTok or television or a performative turn on social media. It's a journey upon which many men are already embarking.

I spoke with Dr. Jorge Rodriguez, a historian of religion who specializes in the history of colonization and how minoritized communities have responded to that threat. That work isn't just professional, however; it's personal. He tells me how, throughout his life, he's received messages of shame around people's bodies. These messages came from extended family, church spaces, but also TV commercials and other forms of media. "I received messages like, 'If you have high blood pressure or diabetes, it's actually a sign that you're morally deficient,'" he says. And this extended to crying as well, "I learned, 'Oh, if you cry, something is wrong.'" All of this has prevented him from listening to what his tears might be trying to communicate. "These issues around my body have been policed as individual failures, moral in nature," he says, "as opposed to asking, 'What is my body trying to tell me?'"

Through years of therapy, however, he's been able to change the way he sees and understands himself. And that means changing how he relates to his gender, too. "As a man in this country,

I've definitely been socialized to first think and then feel," he says. "That has limited my ability to excavate intergenerational patterns of trauma and to develop deeper emotional connections." He says that one of the things he appreciates about tears is that they are such a stark signal that something is happening within himself that he should pay attention to. "Crying is one of the ways that I've started to get in tune with what my body is trying to tell me," he says. "And often it's tapping into a core memory that I haven't excavated, an experience that shaped me." By developing a more intimate somatic relationship, he has been able to cast off some of the shame that society draped around his shoulders.

But crying doesn't just help men become more emotionally attuned to their own bodies; it helps forge social connections as well. Mohammad Mia, who you met at the beginning of the chapter, is a brilliant portrait photographer. Like so many other boys, Mia learned from his parents not to cry. As an adult, however, Mia wants more than that for himself—and for his parents. "Reclaiming vulnerability has been a wonderful yet incredibly difficult process," he confesses. "There was so much hardening to crack open." Part of what helped this process was exploring vulnerability with other men of color. Mia had the opportunity to be an intern at a restorative justice organization, and he reflects, "Access to that space—to other men of color who were able to be emotionally expressive about the grief, the anger, the hopelessness, and the powerlessness they were feeling—really helped me identify and develop a richer vocabulary around emotions."

Learning to cry, Mia says, was integral to this growth. "The tears are definitely a necessary part of that process—the doorway that opens up to other emotions that I haven't had a chance to explore." Stepping across that threshold is scary. For men who have spent so long devoting psychological resources to repressing the depths of our emotions, when we begin to puncture that surface, it can feel like the volume of tears we've dammed might drown us. "Sometimes you worry because you fear you're not equipped to step through this door, or are uncertain about what's on the other side," Mia admits. "But I've found that more often than not, I'm more capable than I believe myself to be. The more I do it, the less scary it becomes."

And the benefits of that work are enormous. "As a photographer, I find that for my subjects, it's an incredibly intimate and vulnerable practice to be in front of the camera," he says. "It's a vulnerability that I learned very quickly I couldn't ask of others without also having the courage to step into it myself." Indeed, sitting for a portrait isn't a bad metaphor for what crying requires more broadly. "Being on the other side of the camera, being intimately close with how you view yourself, your insecurities, it can be a really daunting task," Mia concludes. But if we want to create more gentleness around us, we must turn that lens upon ourselves.

CHAPTER 5

All These Wailing Women

While we often depict men as stoic and dry-eyed, women are described as frequent weepers. From diagnoses of female melancholia to allegations of unpreparedness for politics or corporate leadership, dominant culture has held a deeply sexist presumption that women are prone to dissolve at the slightest provocation. Esther Greenwood, the protagonist in Sylvia Plath's *The Bell Jar*, embodies the stereotype when she is unable to even sit for a photo. "I didn't want my picture taken because I was going to cry," she says. "I didn't know why I was going to cry, but I knew that if anybody spoke to me or looked at me too closely the tears would fly out of my eyes and the sobs would fly out of my throat and I'd cry for a week. I could feel the tears brimming and sloshing in me like water in a glass that is unsteady and too full."

Compared to men, women overall do cry significantly more often. Many studies on crying actually exclude male participants altogether because of the habitual difficulty researchers have in getting men to weep. Still, however, the stereotype of women's copious and regular weeping is more grounded in myth than reality.

Professed links between excessive crying and female anatomy are as old as the field of medicine. We inherit the terms *hysteria* and *melancholia* from none other than Hippocrates himself, who suggested these alleged psychological disturbances were the product of a misaligned uterus. A woman's body, you see, is "physiologically cold and wet and hence prone to putrefaction of the humors (as opposed to the dry and warm male body)." Characteristically, this uterine misalignment could be rectified through a sexually satisfied life within the bounds of marriage. (And if that didn't fix things, there was always "acrid fumigation" of the face and genitals.)

Notably, Cecilia Tossca and her coauthors observe in their research on women, hysteria, and the history of mental health that the "Hippocratic corpus sees woman not as an incomplete male, but as a radically different, inferior body." For thinkers ranging from Aristotle to Galen, male heat and dryness were models of a perfect physical form—an ideal that wet, cold women were fundamentally unable to emulate. Male weeping, by contrast, was depicted then—and now—as effeminizing, a violation of that supposed male dryness. In classical depictions of hell, it's common to find verbose descriptions of men moved to weep by their eternal torture. To the reader, claims religious historian Meghan Henning, "these weeping bodies represent compromised male bodies that are overcome with emotion in a characteristically female way."

While ensuing centuries offered dramatic change to both culture and medical science, the assumption that women were biologically possessed by dramatic and irresistible urges to weep remained. In Renaissance England, for example, women were often referred to as leaky vessels; historian Rachel Vorona Coate writes that women were seen as "unable to control their bodies because of [overflowing] tears, menstrual blood and amniotic fluid." The chaos of these vital forces was too much for a world that prioritized order. Conforming to culture required stifling life.

This mindset treated crying as a destabilizing and problematic impulse, one from which the broader public must be shielded. Coate describes how Victorian customs went as far as to create an entire fashion of "deep mourning" attire, including dramatic, six-foot, double-layered veils to help women conform to "cultural expectations for a 'respectable' mourner." Sadly, the dyes used to color the crepe had the unfortunate side effect of causing skin irritation, headaches, and even death—a dreadful irony by which widows might survive their husbands only to be killed by the grieving.

Few contemporary observers would attribute female weeping to an overproduction of black bile or an imbalance of the humors. Nor do we demand women cloak their unruly tears behind arsenic-laden face drapes. (Though I wouldn't be gobsmacked if "misaligned uterus" made a comeback on Breitbart. And a cursory Google search offers dozens of articles offering to help "hide that you've been crying.")

But many still assume weepiness to be a quintessentially female trait. And we've simply devised new cultural expectations for women—ones that weigh just as heavily as a six-foot veil.

On a 2008 campaign stop in Portsmouth, New Hamphsire, then Senator Hillary Clinton fielded a question from one of her supporters. "My question is very personal," the woman began. "How do you do it? How do you keep upbeat and so wonderful?"

Instead of offering a canned answer, Clinton risked a vulnerable response. "It's not easy," she said. "And I just couldn't do it if I didn't passionately believe it was the right thing to do." A tear glimmered in her eye, as Clinton's usually stoic exterior slipped away for a moment. With a slight catch in her throat, she continued, "I have so many opportunities from this country. I just don't want to see us fall backward."

But rather than retreat to stoicism, she let the moment build. "This is very personal for me," she continued. "It's not just political, it's not just public. I see what's happening and we have to reverse it. Some people think elections are a game—it's about who's up or who's down—it's about our country, and it's about our kids' future."

It was a startlingly human moment, particularly from a candidate who, rightly or wrongly, had developed a reputation for being cold and unfeeling. The public reaction, however, underscored exactly why so many women like Secretary Clinton develop a hardened exterior. On the one hand, she was roundly critiqued for a perceived display of weakness. Writing for the *New York Times*, Maureen Dowd shared the disdain of one of her colleagues. "We are at war. Is that how she'll talk to Kim Jong-Il?" he questioned—as if Clinton would strike the same tone with a foreign dictator.

On the other hand, writing for the *Guardian*, Germaine Greer questioned whether the tears were genuine at all. "Watching Hillary Clinton pretending to get teary-eyed is enough to make me give up shedding tears altogether," Greer writes, labeling Clinton's performance at the campaign stop "a feeble display of emotion." In a scathing critique, Greer suggests the candidate was simply using tears to manipulate her audience. Greer openly yearns for a return to the culture of her youth, when "piping your eye was no more dignified than any other involuntary discharge of bodily fluid, be it snot, blood, seminal fluid or urine." After all, "it takes a lot of self-discipline to be able to remain attractive while weeping."

And while Dowd herself seemed to believe the tears were genuine, she attributes them to self-pity. "What was moving her so deeply was her recognition that the country was failing to grasp how much it needs her," Dowd writes. "In a weirdly narcissistic way, she was crying for us."

What's striking, when watching the Hillary Clinton clip now, are the similarities between this moment and President Obama's weeping, which we looked at in the previous chapter. Neither leader breaks down, and neither's tears are maudlin. But both leaders were willing to reveal that they weren't simply acting out of dispassionate reason. They cared deeply, and it's that caring, they tacitly argue, that makes them a good leader.

The public reaction to their crying, though, reveals the razor's edge upon which women's tears fall. Cry too fervently and it is surely a sign of weakness—a confirmation of the prejudices we already carry about women in power. Hold it back, and you're clearly a phony, a fraud, a fake. Caught between this modern Charybdis and Scylla, some women find no other option than to banish tears entirely. Since we already believe that women are prone to wild and uncontrollable sobs (those wet, cold humors are hard to shake), anything less must certainly be naked calculation. Better to simply refrain from crying. You may be labeled a stone-cold bitch, but perhaps you'll still get to lead.

Most women work in somewhat less high-stakes environments than running for president, but that doesn't mean there aren't similar forces at play. And it's not just fear of judgment by male supervisors or coworkers, either. We've so deftly planted cultural landmines around feminine tears that many women have internalized the conviction that frequent crying correlates to less competence.

My wife, Erin, used to work as an editor at a popular women's media website. The corporate culture proudly embraced a #girlboss feminism, and almost all her coworkers were women. But that didn't erase the stigma of an office sob. The shame and perceived weakness of open crying lingered. Every single one of her former coworkers I talked with for this book had several stories about breaking down in tears at the office (it wasn't a healthy workplace). But they all reported regarding a near-universal experience as if it were a personal failing.

One staircase, in particular, was known as the place to hide when crying—as if hiding the anguish and frustration of being undervalued and abused by their corporation was what it meant to be strong. One of Erin's former coworkers is Emma Lord, now a *New York Times* bestselling novelist. "I definitely did not feel comfortable crying openly," she remembers. "If it was going to happen, everybody had a designated spot—or multiple spots, because sometimes you would go to your spot and there would already be someone crying in it, so you would have to find another one."

Given the way the company publicly positioned itself—as a feminist corrective to patriarchal media spaces—Lord notes the irony of both the lack of tolerance for tears and the hostile culture that provoked them in the first place. "Most of my professional career beyond college has been working in female-dominated spaces, and every single one of them touted this philosophy of 'we support women, don't be afraid to cry, don't be afraid to express yourself,'" she says. "They'd say, 'We want to hear you, we want to support you.' And we would laugh, because we'd publish articles touting these philosophies that we absolutely weren't following ourselves." Eventually, after years of performing this charade, Lord says, it all began to feel surreal. "It was almost like writing professional fan fiction: 'Wouldn't it be nice if this kind of office space existed, and wouldn't it be nice if it was us.' But it never was."

This type of tear-punishing environment didn't start with predominantly female offices, Lord is quick to note; it trickled down from patriarchal spaces that still dictate what it means to be "professional" in our collective imaginary. "We were trying to both create a space for ourselves but also mimic the success of what was going on around us," she says. "So it brings in this workplace culture where you're expected to behave a certain way." And it's not just externally imposed pressure, either. After working in these kinds of environments for extended periods, we begin to internalize those values. "Even as someone who's frustrated that I can't cry in an office," she confesses, "I find myself in moments where I don't feel sympathy for a person who cries: 'You could have found a perfectly good stairwell like the rest of us.'"

The stigma against crying at work persists in no small part because it allows people who exploit their employees to pretend everything is fine. Open weeping disrupts that lie and shatters the capitalistic artifice. Interestingly, while many of the men I've interviewed expressed a hesitance to cry because they expected retribution—being derided as weak or less of a man—Lord says that much of her resistance to open crying comes from a fear of burdening other people. "You don't want anyone to have to take on the emotional labor of you crying," she says. "It comes from a place of guilt. They have their own things to focus on, their own stresses that are probably making *them* cry."

Some women do forcibly suppress their tears because they fear retribution. The social costs levied against women of color who cry at the office are even more pernicious and pervasive than they are for white women. Alex Love is a diversity, equity, and inclusion consultant for some of the country's largest companies. They previously worked at Vice Media. No matter whether you work at a trendy media outlet or a multinational conglomerate, Love says, crying can be a treacherous minefield. "Because we do live under patriarchy and white dominant culture in the workplace, emotions in general are not given space or time," they tell me. "Crying is stigmatized in the office because it's feminized, and therefore bad, like all feminine emotions in the office."

This general proscription against tears intersects with—and is intensified by—the racism nonwhite workers experience. "As a Black person trying to navigate respectability politics, knowing how racism exists, you're not going to see me crying, because I have to prove something to you," Love says. On occasions when Love did cry at work, earlier in their career, they were shocked by white coworkers' lack of empathy. After high-profile police murders of Black people, for example, "there was a lack of understanding about why the sadness and grief exists. . . . People would say, 'As a white person, I'm not upset when other white people are murdered on the news.'" Love says the office mood was entirely different, however, after President Trump was elected. "It was fascinating watching the white women in the office cry all day," Love observes. "The allowance of all of these white women crying about this election . . . yielded a very different response, and a very different permission of vulnerability."

Love's words offer yet another reminder that, although almost everyone feels pressure against crying at work, we do not all feel that pressure equally. "It's an extension of racism," Love says bluntly. "The complete disregard of Black emotion outside of rage is part of the same ideology of Black people not having feelings or emotions. It's aligned with portrayal of Black people . . . as animalistic, unable to contain that rage and anger—instead of understanding that a whole group of people are living under oppression on a day-to-day basis."

The different reactions to tears depending on folks' social location only amplifies people's fear about being fully and authentically themselves at work. And when people feel anxious and unsure about the potential reaction to their tears, the simplest solution is to hold them in. A degree of personal alienation becomes the cost of doing business.

While many women still feel hemmed in by these sexist constraints, others are roundly rejecting what they were handed. They are using tears to demand a world that enables and encourages a full range of emotional expression.

Brittany Ramos DeBarros is a veteran and antiwar organizer who was running for Staten Island's congressional seat while I was writing this book. We met working with the Poor People's Campaign—a modern revival of the political campaign Martin Luther King Jr. was organizing when he was assassinated—and, from the moment we first spoke, I was enraptured. She combines deep knowledge of our military's domestic and foreign abuses with fervent belief in our ability to change them. When she claims that a different world is possible and describes how it might come to be, I believe her. Curious whether tears contributed to this moral clarity, I ring her up. Her voice is energetic and forceful when she confirms how integrating her emotional life was a pre-requisite for following her convictions.

Brittany doesn't remember receiving much explicit instruction not to cry when she was growing up, but she definitely remembers those messages being targeted at boys. At that time in the 1990s, in the throes of girl-power energy, this instilled in her a resolve to be just as stoic as the boys around her were. "I remember the Mia Hamm *Got Milk* commercial, where the song in the background was 'Anything you can do, I can do better,'" she tells me. "I'm seeing boys be shamed for crying because it's not tough, but at the same time I'm thinking, 'I'm a girl and I'm tough too. I can be as tough as you are.'" Even though it wasn't intended for her, DeBarros internalized the message that strength and tears were mutually exclusive.

When she enlisted in the army, she received that same message on steroids—jacked up by the incredible pressure of serving as a woman and wed to the full oppressive might of the Defense Department. "I *definitely* didn't feel like I could cry openly in the military," she laughs, "especially as an officer. I had a very firm personal rule that I used to repeat to myself: no crying in uniform." Despite these intentions, she says, "I cried in my uniform all the time! What that rule really meant was, 'not in front of other people.' I couldn't afford to be seen as this highly feminized leader who was soft and didn't have the grit to lead in a military context. I didn't want my logic to be dismissed because I also had emotions and tears."

But internalized shame over crying often channels our anguish into private lacrimal rivers. When we're ashamed of crying, we don't necessarily cry less often; we just learn to do it by ourselves. DeBarros marvels now at "the number of times I cried alone in my office, in my car, after drill just from the sheer overwhelm of how fucked up everything was." She recalls now lying in a tent, "days away from dropping into a combat zone, and just trying to cry silently in my sleeping bag, so that people wouldn't hear me."

But crying is never just about crying. Brittany's experience was indicative of a deeper sickness, one she says undergirds so much of the dehumanization and atrocities committed by our military. "You're implicitly taught that, when you put your uniform on, you take your humanity off, and then you come home at the end of the day and you take your uniform off and you put your humanity back on," she observes. "Your humanity is a liability rather than a strength."

But the deep feeling she tried so hard to extinguish is what ultimately saved her. "I couldn't set aside my human compassion and connection with the Afghan people when I was there," she says. As a leader tasked with developing strategic communications, she spent extended time with the communities the US was occupying. Instead of cultivating emotional detachment, she found herself asking questions such as, "How does this Afghan village leader feel? How does this mother feel? What have they gone through?" This broader lens widened how she viewed their lives beyond the narrow perspective the US military wants for its soldiers. "The presence of emotion, my inability or refusal to take that humanity off when I put my uniform on," she recalls, "created the conditions for me to see so clearly that we were not operating in alignment with justice, despite what I had hoped and believed when I went there."

While still a captain in the army, DeBarros began to speak out against the occupation. In July 2018, when she was called up for two weeks of active orders, she prescheduled fourteen days of tweets telling the truth about the Defense Department's actions. Posting partisan political opinions on social media while one is on duty goes against army protocols for commissioned officers, but there was nothing partisan about what she posted—just publicly available facts. While this plan cleverly found a loophole around that ban, it quickly drew the attention of both conservative media and the military itself.

One suspects, however, that it was less the fact that she was using social media that stoked their ire and more the contents of the tweets themselves. "At the current rate, the US drops a bomb every 12 minutes," one of Brittany's tweets read. "Defense corporations made contributions to 496 of 525 members of Congress in 2018," read another. A third proclaimed the number of Afghan civilians killed or injured by US forces: 4,732 in 2009, 8,019 in 2017. "Has 16+ years of occupation made them safer?" it asked.

The tears Brittany wept privately for the Afghan people she now wept openly for the world to see. And unlike critiques of the military solely through the lens of what it costs the US—the financial price of war, the number of service members who die—DeBarros squarely centered the people who suffer most acutely: the people who live in countries we invade. Speaking with the *Guardian* after President Biden withdrew our troops, she was painfully honest: "We were trying to build something in our image without real buy-in or leadership from Afghan people," she said. "The US military is an institution designed to do as much violence as possible. You can't use it and tweak it a little and act like it's going to give you a different result."

Now Brittany Ramos DeBarros is running for Congress to bring a desperately needed antiwar voice to a House marked by decades-long, bipartisan commitment to bloodshed. And she wears her emotions proudly as a strength, not a weakness. "There's a real dynamic of intellectualizing the issues we face—and I'm not coming from a place of anti-intellectualism," she says. Yet she refuses to be complicit in decision-making "divorced from the suffering we're actually talking about."

Cultural prohibitions against crying and deep emotion draw so much power from the way we police ourselves. Sometimes the most direct recourse is to wield tears themselves as confrontation. DeBarros hopes to embody this through policymaking that grows out of the tears she shed and the tears of the victims of US military incursions.

Meanwhile, in the Netherlands, one graduate student embraced the concept of tears as confrontation—literally.

Academia has long been an environment that breaks people down under the guise of making them stronger. New generations of students have begun to question the wisdom of this bargain. In particular, disregard for students' emotional health has come under fire as undermining academic growth and facilitating the kinds of predatory behavior that has long lurked in ivory towers.

Yi-Fei Chen was a Taiwanese student who emigrated to Design Academy Eindhoven in the Netherlands to pursue her master's degree. Throughout her program, she felt trapped by the school's high-pressure environment. But as an exchange student and someone who grew up in a cultural context that discouraged disagreeing with your professors, she didn't feel comfortable pushing back against an often-unrealistic workload. Things finally came to a boiling point midway through her second year, when she again found herself overwhelmed by her expected tasks. In a confrontation with one of her professors, Chen remembers, "I was too emotional to control myself. I could not hold my tears, so I cried. I turned my back to the others, because I did not want people to see me crying."

Rather than be ashamed of these tears, however, Chen chose to wield them in protest against the educational environment that made her cry in the first place. Using her design skills, she invented an elaborate brass gun that collects tears as they roll down her cheek, uses compressed air to freeze them, and then fires the frozen drops from a long delicate barrel.

As performance art, the tear gun creates a striking image: Chen as part cyberpunk goddess, part mad scientist. Its elegance is matched only by its power, and the project immediately became an international news story. Millions were drawn to the image and oddity of this emotionally healthy Bond villain. But as much as the gun itself was an object of fascination, Yi-Fei's story resonated equally deeply. By refusing to cry silently and out of sight, she gave countless students voice to express their own anguish. She also got the last laugh. At her graduation, Yi-Fei was offered the chance to "shoot" the department chair with her frozen tears—and gladly took it.

Taking such an intimate and vulnerable process and transforming it into a weapon is a peculiar irony. But what options remain when emotions are stifled and those in power reject them entirely? Chen's artistic proclamation rejects this accursed silence: if you will not honor my humanity then, damn it, I will transform my weeping into something you cannot ignore. My pain will not go unnoticed. My tears have weight, shape, and heft. If you do not make room for them, they will sting.

Chen is part of a broader wave of women who are break-ing customs that were never designed to help them flourish. We don't prohibit all emotional expression in our workplaces. Delight in our successes and anxieties about upcoming projects are often welcomed. Even anger, while not an optimal energy to bring into a room, finds open expression when problems arise. Yet somehow we're deemed less competent when we openly cry in a meeting than we are when we berate a coworker. Put bluntly, men have designed the rules that govern professional emotional expression, and most men are more comfortable with yelling than with tears. But as the gender balance shifts in workplaces, these customs are shifting, too.

It's tempting to portray this change as an entirely new devel-opment, but women's tears were not always associated with fra-gility. This double bind into which we place women—powerless when emotional, suspicious when emotionless—is actually a modern contrivance.

Consider again that story at the very heart of the biblical resur-rection: Mary Magdalene weeping over Jesus at the empty tomb. Regardless about what you believe about the resurrection of Jesus, what's abundantly clear from this story is that the ancient audience did not consider Mary's weeping to be weak. To the contrary, it is offered as evidence of the depth of her devotion—*the reason she is chosen* to be the very first Christian to proclaim the good news of God's victory over death. We know this is true because, just a few verses earlier, Simon Peter and another dis-ciple visit the tomb and see the bands of cloth where Jesus lay.

They, however, simply leave the empty tomb; Jesus does not, at that point, appear to them. It is only when Mary Magdalene shows the power of her love that Jesus reveals himself.

And the power of wailing women isn't just constrained to the Bible, either. In various African cultures, there is a long tradition of mourners who are hired to weep at funerals. Historic accounts of this practice date back to ancient Egypt, and such mourning practices still thrive in many countries. Speaking with BBC Africa, Ami Dokli, a Ghanaian professional mourner, observes that "some people don't know how to cry." In order to properly grieve the dead, she and other women use the power of their own tears to unlock those frozen within others. In these contexts, it is the *failure* to weep that is perceived as weakness. Lack of tears, not the tears themselves, is the thing to be rectified.

Obviously, weeping over the crucified or at a loved one's funeral differs from crying at the office or on the campaign trail. But a significant part of that difference is the way that we've constructed professional life as an environment divorced from the daily rhythms of living. That, however, is not a divinely ordained state of affairs. In fact, the ways we pretend labor can be wholly separated from the rest of our lives is a significant reason our workplaces can be so traumatic. The expectation that we simply endure continuous harm without letting it permeate the office walls is a holdover from the pathological masculinity that shaped them. It's time to let that sickness go.

As more women lead professional teams and shatter patriarchal paradigms, their leadership can create an environment in which people of every gender feel more comfortable crying. While I became much more comfortable crying in my personal life when I was in seminary, it wasn't until I worked as a minister for Middle Church that I was able to openly cry at work. When

I worked as an editor at Time Inc., I loved the job but I never would have felt comfortable crying at the office. Instead, at the end of a particularly hard day, my boss would break out the bottle of whiskey he kept in his bottom drawer—a more traditional though decidedly less healthy coping mechanism.

But our senior minister at Middle Church, Rev. Dr. Jacqui Lewis, creates an atmosphere where open crying isn't just accepted but welcomed. We will never be able to cast off deeply ingrained proscriptions against crying without intentional effort, and Jacqui deliberately constructs space for emotional processing. We frequently have meetings designed to accomplish nothing beyond building a container to hold our feelings in community. And this isn't just restricted to work-related feelings, either. A healthy workplace understands that its employees are people, deeply affected by the world outside the office.

This was particularly true in the pandemic, when grief was a constant companion. Sobbing on a video call is an odd experience. There's a sterility to the little squares, and you can't place a comforting hand on someone's shoulder. Your own emotions seem to slip into the ether—disappearing into ones and zeros you hope will be caught by another heart. Yet those moments were salvation. They rescued me from the isolation of my walls and tethered me to people I love but could not embrace. And they enabled our team to persevere through years that strained so many churches to their breaking point.

This is the ultimate failure of leadership styles that view collective grieving as wasted time: they don't grasp the fact that people do their best work when they feel held and cared for. An hour spent crying together may facilitate another week of productivity. Hopefully this trend of supporting employees in their fullest emotional expressions will continue as more leaders witness the benefits of an emotionally supportive workplace. If there's one thing professional culture respects, it's results. And bosses who lead through abuse will be forced to answer for why their teams are not as productive as those who lead with compassion and empathy, not to mention why they're unable to attract and retain top-caliber employees.

While these shifting norms are certainly a welcome development, they are not equally distributed among all people. The positive trends in this chapter are still largely restricted to white-collar employment. And even in workplaces that tolerate or celebrate a wider range of emotionality, racism constrains equal enjoyment of these benefits. Too often, our culture is only comfortable with weeping when tears fall down white cheeks.

CHAPTER 6

Caste against Crying

In 2016, Charlotte police watched Keith Lamont Scott leave his car to walk to his apartment. They claimed he had a gun and decided he posed an "imminent deadly threat." North Carolina, it should be noted, is an open-carry state. Officers immediately drew their weapons. CBS News describes how dashboard camera footage shows Scott, in response to the drawn guns, "slowly backing away from his SUV with his hands down." His effort to calm this situation was unsuccessful. "Four shots are heard in quick succession, and he crumples to the ground mortally wounded."

Days after the killing, at a city council meeting, nine-year-old Zianna Oliphant took the microphone, tears streaming down her face. "We shouldn't have to feel like this," she said bluntly. "We do this because we need to have rights." At this juncture, Mayor Jennifer Roberts had to quiet hecklers outraged by the notion that a Black girl would demand her rights. Undeterred by the loud boos, Oliphant continued sobbing. "I can't stand how we're treated. It's a shame that our mothers and fathers are killed and we can't see them anymore. It's a shame that we have to go to the graveyard and bury them."

Her anguish, her community's pain, and well-documented video weren't enough to bring Scott's case to trial. Despite the crime scene evidence, District Attorney Andrew Murray concluded the officers "acted lawfully" and thus refused to bring charges. And Zianna Oliphant learned that American grief has a race-based exchange rate. While our culture has dedicated both laws and lynchings to white girls' tears, Zianna's were summarily discarded by the state.

More than that, Zianna learned her tears will anger people in her community. Think about the racism that moves someone to jeer at a sobbing child who is begging for the very right to life and liberty her Constitution promises. To layer that festering rage on her already crushing sorrow is a particular kind of American savagery.

But thankfully, Zianna also heard the roar and cheer of the community around her: the adults who rose applauding as she finished, shouting, "No justice, no peace." Blackness in America has always been, in part, a story of people showing clear and intentional wounds to a country hell-bent on ignoring them. It has meant living in the communal hope that the magnitude of that grief and the power of the ensuing lament will move sinful hands toward just action. Oliphant strode into that story as she summed up its clear indictment: "We have tears, and we shouldn't have tears."

Reasons white society refuses to hear that cry are as old as the cry itself. In his 1781 treatise *Notes on the State of Virginia*, Thomas Jefferson writes, "Love seems with [Black people] to be more an eager desire, than a tender delicate mixture of sentiment and sensation. Their griefs are transient. Those numberless afflictions . . . are less felt, and sooner forgotten with them." This conviction—that Black people possess stunted emotional lives, that they feel joy and sorrow alike less deeply than white people—is as foundational to this country as the words Jefferson penned in his more celebrated documents. It has been used, time and again, to justify racist violence. It still abounds.

In her essay about medical racism for *The 1619 Project*, Linda Villarosa observes that "present-day doctors fail to sufficiently treat the pain of black adults and children for many medical issues." This is a disturbing but also unsurprising result, given the shameful fact that a survey of 222 white medical students and residents revealed that "half of them endorsed at least one myth about physiological differences between Black people and white people, including that Black people's nerve endings are less sensitive than white people's." When some of the most educated members of white society imagine entire communities to be less susceptible to pain and harm, it should shock no one that Zianna Oliphant's tears are discarded. Black people's weeping is too often treated as a mere simulacrum of genuine sorrow.

The truth, however, is that Black cultures in America embrace a depth of feeling—a breadth between pain and pleasure— that often dwarfs that of their white counterparts. The brutality and violence inflicted on generations birthed sweeping artistic responses that both process that suffering and foster fierce joy to resist its abuses.

Black spirituals, for example, show that potent mixture of grief and resilience. White observers often deride weeping as weak sentimentality, and too often white analysis of Black art focuses on trauma without understanding the transformational power nestled inside it. It's a double-edged dehumanization—one that diminishes the depths of pain while simultaneously ignoring the prophetic claim those words make on all people. This type of white-rendered history ignores how enslavement indicts whiteness.

The powerful lament "Sometimes I Feel Like a Motherless Child" aches and groans in ways you cannot escape noticing. But white listeners have too often acted as if this is an abstract, extractable pain, rather than the anguish of the auction block that left countless people literally motherless. Yet while spirituals often responded to slavery's trauma, the brutality of white society is not their focus. The theological heart of the spirituals is the liberation God was enacting in and among Black people. This is a grief that simultaneously demands freedom.

In his masterpiece *The Spirituals and the Blues*, Rev. Dr. James H. Cone highlights how, in the spiritual "Nobody Knows the Trouble I've Seen," the lyrics offer both a sophisticated response to theodicy (the question of why an omnipotent God could allow suffering); a wailing to express that pain; and the proclamation of a love that could end it. "The 'Glory, Hallelujah' was not a denial of trouble," he writes. "It was an affirmation of faith: God is the companion of sufferers and *trouble* is not the last word on human existence."

In that understanding, these moans are not only the expression of people groaning beneath unjust and unimaginable suffering; they are also an inextricable part of the movement that can end it. "Far from being songs of passive resignation," Cone concludes, "the spirituals are Black freedom songs which emphasize Black liberation as consistent with divine revelation." Weeping, likewise, cannot always be understood as purely emotional expression. When tied to faith in a future where God will dry every eye of tears they should not need to shed, weeping is an eschatological foretaste for how that world will feel.

In the dozens of interviews I conducted for this book, a pattern emerged: Black folks I spoke with were far more likely than their white counterparts to report having grown up in homes that encouraged crying, and they more frequently described memories of communal tears. Many white people I spoke with couldn't remember *ever* being part a collective weeping experience; even funerals were largely dry-eyed, beyond perhaps the deceased's immediate family and friends. This does not happen by accident. For many Black Americans, crying isn't just a mark of a healthy emotional life; it's necessary for survival.

"The appropriate time to cry was often," Rev. Dr. Jacqui Lewis says, quick to share memories of her childhood. "For joy, for being deeply moved, for grief. We saw Dad cry a lot. And we saw Mom cry a lot. There was a lot of expressiveness in my family." It wasn't just her experience at home, however, that instilled a belief in the importance and power of crying. When attending New Friendship Missionary Baptist Church in Chicago as a young child, she recalls an "off-the-chain charismatic expression of faith: shouting that might be weeping also. Dance that might include weeping. The organist playing, 'If you're giving up your sins, come to the altar!' and people crying as they walk up." Dr. Lewis tells me she would watch "people running the aisles singing 'Hallelujah!'" and she would pray to God, "I want that Spirit. I longed for it."

After her family began to attend a Black Presbyterian church, exuberant worship gave way to a more contemplative style. But communal weeping, she says, remained a defining feature of what it meant to come together in faith. "There we got lots of quiet and tears," she says with a smile; "*lots* of tears. The preacher is preaching and the organist's face is streaming." And she is quick to name how being surrounded by crying invited her own.

"In that way that someone's laughter can make you laugh," she says, "I found a permission to cry. The thought of my mother saying, 'This bread means God will love you. This cup means God will never leave you': it still makes me cry today." But it wasn't just her experience. "I could see my little brothers crying," she says, "You could see little kids watching: what is happening right now? Everybody is crying, it's like that holy scene in *Beloved* of Baby Suggs pulling everybody into the clearing: you look around and you see adults crying. You don't know why they're crying, but you start crying too because your heart is pricked."

But you can't detach the emotional education she and other Black children received inside of the church from the political education they received outside of it, Dr. Lewis says. "When you're that young, it's hard to separate what you've experienced and what you've seen. You've seen replays of King's speeches. You've seen people weeping at the funeral. You've seen Mamie Till crying in *Jet Magazine*." In the same way that adults were carrying those burdens inside the walls of the church to lift them up to God, kids were learning how to live and fight for justice in this country without becoming numb.

"Sociologically, physiologically, biologically, or psychologically: we have come over a way that with tears has been watered," Dr. Lewis says. This way of tears isn't just something that Black children learn about in a history book; it is passed down between generations. "It is the archetypal memory of, 'I am standing on the block, being sold away from my mother,'" she says. "I'm not there, but I'm always there. I'm always there." The legacy of slavery and Jim Crow isn't ethereal; it's inscribed in the very landscape. "You go to Montgomery, and you go to the Equal Justice Initiative museum, and you look down the river. You don't have to see a picture to picture a little baby being ripped out of their mother's arm, or fathers being sold away, or children standing by the fencepost watching someone get whipped," she says, her face grave. "All of that is etched into the soul of Black America and into my soul as a Black American. The reasons for tears are plentiful."

Crying is not just a product of unjust suffering, though, she says; it becomes a fount of resilience. "Weeping together bonds us," Dr. Lewis notes. "How else can you make it except by embracing the ability to cry?"

This emotional wellspring makes the ways white culture has dismissed Black tears even more insidious and insulting. "When Thomas Jefferson describes Black people as having transient grief, fleeting grief, not really grief at all—it's such a dehumanizing lie," Dr. Lewis notes. And the dehumanization is very much the point. If you truly reckon with someone's tears—if you confront and acknowledge the enormity of their pain and grief—it becomes far harder to justify exploitation and violence. "It allows you to imagine you haven't wounded that person," she says. "It's easier to 'thingify' somebody if you can't picture them as vulnerable enough to cry. It allows you to imagine that they're not wound-able, which is to say that they're an object. And then you don't have to deal with their feelings."

We reveal much by who we consider worthy of empathy. There was a moment at the sentencing of police officer Kim Potter that devastatingly embodied this dynamic. After a jury found officer Potter guilty for killing Daunte Wright at a traffic stop, the judge decided to discard the state guidelines and sentence Potter to only two years in prison. As she explained her decision, Judge

Regina Chu encouraged those in the courtroom to put themselves in Potter's shoes. "Officer Kimberly Potter was trying to
do the right thing," Chu said, her eyes welling with tears. Potter,
the judge said, "made a mistake that ended tragically, she never
intended to hurt anyone."

Evidently, that ethos of mercy only extends to the white
police officer guilty of murder, and not the sobs of a broken-
hearted family crying out for justice after their son was killed.
At the same sentencing hearing, Daunte's mother, Katie Wright,
asked the judge to hold Potter accountable. "She took our baby
boy with a single gunshot through his heart," Wright said, "and
she shattered mine."

Despite the repeated violence of a country that refuses to see
or honor Black tears, that weeping continues. It's precisely the
tenacity of Black grief that continues to provoke suppression and
violence. "It's subversive, the ability to cry together," Dr. Lewis
tells me. "It's a magic and a power that nobody can take away.
'The world didn't give it to me, the world can't take it away,' is
what we sing about joy—but it's true for crying too."

Those tears aren't just an outpouring of emotion or a need for
catharsis; they're a full-throated rejection of a country that has
tried to steal Black people's control over their bodies. In *Stand
Your Ground: Black Bodies and the Justice of God*, her fabulous book
responding to the lynching of Trayvon Martin, the Very Rev. Dr.
Kelly Brown Douglas notes that "Black people under slavery did
not have the rights to possess their bodies." She outlines how the
ensuing history of vagrancy laws, redlining, Jim Crow, and mass
incarceration were all attempts to restrict Black people's ability to
move through white spaces. "Free Black bodies have to be guilty
of something," she writes, and whiteness has been relentlessly
creative in building an ever-changing cage. All of this is an effort

to do what was once accomplished through overt legislation: publicly define Black people as less than fully human.

And that's precisely why Black tears are treated as a threat, Dr. Douglas tells me. "Crying is a sign of a person's humanity," she says. In a country where "Black people are still seen as animals, as beasts, if tears are a sign of one's humanity, then heaven forbid this be a sign of Black humanity."

Even knowing this history though, she says, doesn't lessen the pain when Black tears are summarily dismissed. "I remember the personal conversations I had with Trayvon Martin's parents," she says. "Trayvon's father thought that, at the trial for his son's killer, the other women on the jury would relate to Trayvon's mother and see that Trayvon was some mother's child. However, he was astounded when that didn't happen. Her tears were discounted because they couldn't see Trayvon as a son, as a human being, and they couldn't see her that way either." This is white supremacy: a culture that holds more empathy for George Zimmerman's unrepentant violence than Sybrina Fulton's tears. "It's like saying to his mother, 'Why are you crying over *that* boy for?'" Dr. Douglas observes.

Faced with this onslaught of dehumanization, Dr. Douglas sees collective weeping as an affirmation of Black personhood. "Communal acts of grieving, joy or resistance and anger: it's an affirmation of one's humanity," she says. "It's not always, if ever, safe to do that in a society and world so riven with antiblackness." And so Black community becomes the space to live full and abundant life. "There's no recognition of Black pain, of Black grief, no room for Black anger or Black rage," she says. But in a moment of collective tears, "you look at that other Black person to say, 'It's okay. I feel what you're feeling. I know what you're feeling.' You don't need the words to express that."

History shows that this saline affirmation of Black humanity threatens a social order predicated on oppression. "Communal grief, particularly in the context of funerals, is also communal protest," Dr. Douglas says. "It's protest to say that these people *did* matter, that these were sacred lives, and that you will not get away with it. It's protest against that which denies the sacredness of Black bodies and the sacredness of Black lives."

Change begins, she says, when people "begin to become proximate with the people [they have] so dehumanized so [they] can see their humanity." And there's nothing more intimate than sitting with someone's tears. Once you've acknowledged the depth of their feeling—the fundamental overlap between someone else's emotional life and your own—it is much harder to see them as an object. Like the historic Civil Rights signs, tears proclaim, "I am a human."

The potent combination of rage and mourning threatens to unsettle structural violence, and the people who profit from that violence would very much rather it did not. So send in the tanks! Deploy the tear gas! Order officers to beat and maim, to cudgel freedom with clubs and strangle wailing lamentation before it can be heard by masses lulled into sinful indifference. The blues project a defiant, dissonant note against a soundscape of carefully cultivated Muzak. Protest shuts down streets intended for commerce, shattering the carefully cultivated illusion that all is well. When America criminalizes Black grief, it seeks to silence a consistently prophetic voice. That is, of course, the intent.

Yet, another defining characteristic of Black resistance is the refusal to be silenced. Denmark Vesey and Nat Turner faced death before acquiescing to evil. Marchers on the Edmund Pettus Bridge were unequivocal: our pain will be heard. Time and again, systems that try to extinguish Black humanity confront resilience that shows the very best of what it means to be human: a love that demands freedom and will not settle for chains—no matter what form they take. If the middle passage could not drown those tears, a burgeoning fascist state sure as hell won't strongarm silence.

But outright condemnation and suppression isn't America's only response to Black tears. Often, the country has been content to ignore them entirely. If Black prophetic grief has been a functional conscience for the nation, a sizable percentage of the population has expressed an unequivocal preference for numbness—reacting only when the pain expressed becomes unavoidable.

The fury against critical race theory in schools has been precisely this kind of reaction. For decades, schools were content to teach curricula that minimized or wholeheartedly ignored the central role white supremacy has played in American life. With reading lists whiter than *A Prairie Home Companion* and a Eurocentric lens for history, you don't need laws that explicitly forbid teaching about racism.

Amid waves of public grief following the lynchings of George Floyd, Breonna Taylor, and Ahmaud Arbery, however, schools faced renewed and sustained pressure to integrate antiracist resources and works of Black literature into their curricula. Initially, the reaction was a surge in the purchase of books like Ibram X. Kendi's *How to Be an Antiracist* and Beverly Daniel Tatum's *Why Are All the Black Kids Sitting Together in the Cafeteria?* However, that initial fervor quickly transformed into a reactionary fury as white schoolchildren and their parents began to experience the attendant guilt that comes from any honest examination of our history. It's such a telling swing in sentiment, America in microcosm: all of a sudden centuries of carefully documented harm (and its ongoing legacy) mattered less than the way it made white people feel.

In January 2022, Florida governor Ron DeSantis voiced his support for a bill that takes this dynamic to farcical new heights. The "Individual Freedom" bill would make it illegal for education in schools or workplaces to make anyone "feel discomfort, guilt, anguish, or any other form of psychological distress on account of his or her race." Crucially, the bill makes no exceptions if the provocation for that discomfort is simply an unpleasant truth; the only thing that matters is whether it distresses the white psyche. The same government that enacted a brutal caste system is now claiming that asking people to wrestle with that history goes beyond the pale.

When I talk with DJ, producer, and diversity, equity, and inclusion consultant Olivia (Liv) Minick, she is quick to differentiate between the way her parents held and embraced her crying in her home or in their Black church, and how her parents reacted to the same emotional expression at the predominantly white schools she attended. "I cried all the time growing up," she remembers, "and I was used to seeing my mom cry a lot. I always felt that there were lots of tears that were healthy." In everything from falling off her bike to seeing church members catch the Spirit or crying joyfully at a family gathering, she says her parents "didn't make me feel like I was being too sensitive when I was crying about anything."

This attitude shifted, however, particularly with her father, when she began attending mostly white private schools. In those settings, she recalls, "there was an unspoken expectation that I not cry. My dad would push me to be tough in those spaces." Indeed there was such an emphasis on eliminating any vulnerability that she says she actually became a bully for some time. "He told me, 'If anyone ever hits you first, or steps to you in a messed-up way, you can hit them.'"

While Minick says she had to outgrow and overcome that advice, she very much sees it as an expression of her father's care. He knew that her tears wouldn't be treated in the same way as her white classmates'. "Even though now, for me, I don't think that's healthy," she reflects. "I know that was his expression of love." No parent wants to see their child experience harm, and this was his way of trying to shield her from it: "He didn't want me to be a target."

What pains her most, she says, is that in significant ways her dad was right. As she got older, she noticed that when she did cry it wasn't held with the same tenderness, or even basic fairness, by the school administration. She tells me about the time she got suspended from her high school basketball team by a racist coach. "A white friend got me a penis lollypop and I, like a dumbass, was chilling in the waiting room of our gym before an away game, and I was sucking on the penis." Her coach saw her but didn't say anything. He did, however, report the incident to the athletic director, who summoned Minick and her mom into the office the following day. The athletic director asked her where she had obtained the phallic candy, and she admitted her friend had given it to her as a joke.

The friend and her mom were then called in. Both girls sat in the office crying, embarrassed and horrified at a silly gag that had gotten way out of hand. The coach and athletic director informed Minick that she would be suspended from the basketball team. Her friend, however, received no punishment at all.

As she recalls the incident, Minick reflects on how painful it was to see her genuine remorse so casually discarded while her friend's tears garnered leniency. "Even though I was crying in the room with the director, it didn't matter," she says. "Your tears don't matter."

And so a girl who was openly expressive and emotional at home learned that she needed to compartmentalize and conceal those parts of herself from a broader world that would not honor them. "I learned not to show my feelings," she says. "I was a class clown, a bully; there was a lot of masking that I did. So many ways to hide how truly sensitive I was."

As we saw in chapter 3, research suggests that communication is one of crying's core purposes. But if tears are habitually ignored (while still carrying all the inherent vulnerability and culturally assigned weakness) is it any wonder that some Black people report extinguishing them entirely—or, at the very least, suppressing them in white-dominant spaces?

Eventually Minick found a way to integrate her innate sensitivity into a form she could safely express while holding the fullness of her feeling: music. "For a lot of us, especially those of us who learn our tears aren't good," she says, "the music becomes the tears." Music let her embody her joy, sorrow, hope, and loss in a medium that both communicated them to the world and offered tenderness to herself. "Those pitches, those resonances, those tones, they're a balm."

Minick traces the casual disregard for Black suffering to the same period that birthed the spirituals and blues. "It all traces back to slavery," she says. "It didn't matter if we cried, it didn't matter if we pleaded or begged not to have to go through trauma, we weren't seen as human beings. And in serious ways, we still aren't." While our nation may be temporally removed from enslavement (setting aside for the moment the ways slavery has deftly morphed into new forms), its psychological inheritance remains potent. Generations of white people seeing Black people as literal property and capital powerfully shapes modern perception. "Experiencing the face of oppression, living in a world like that, white people have been so conditioned not to care," Minick notes. "It's easy to become numb to it all."

Actor Kaliswa Brewster, who plays roles on television shows like *Billions* and *God Friended Me*, expresses similar ambivalence about navigating a cultural landscape that isn't always hospitable to tears. Growing up as the child of immigrants, she saw her parents' concern about how vulnerability can invite harm. "My parents saw crying as a sign of weakness and, especially when it was done in public, as a display that something's wrong," she says. "Being okay and having everybody think that we were okay was really important, even as my parents were figuring out how to be here." Like Minick, even though she might choose to raise children differently, Brewster sees this as an extension of her parents' love. "On the one hand it can seem really harsh," she concedes. "On the other hand, it was a protection: this girl needs to be strong, she can't be falling apart all the time, and if she is falling apart she certainly can't display it, because that'll be a sign of weakness to the world."

As she got older, she began to realize that her parents' fears were very much grounded. Even when she feels like crying, she often holds back, "trying not to appear weak or incompetent, or not show that I'm hurt by a comment someone has made or an assumption that I'm whatever based on my race—not qualified, not good." While this may pay professional dividends, on a personal level she says that it's exhausting to constantly perform for whiteness. "It takes a lot to trust," she confesses, "because I don't necessarily assume when I'm in white spaces that someone is actually seeing me, hearing me, or taking me seriously."

As an actor, she is particularly attuned to the psychic cost of continually inhabiting this role. At times, it feels like a betrayal. "It feels like upholding a make-believe world. I can know what I really feel and what my actual thoughts are, but constantly having to cover them, shape them, make them more acceptable can take you down a road that you're not really trying to travel. And then you start asking yourself, 'What am I really here to do?'" At the same time, it's not as easy as just deciding to be authentic all the time, she says, when the world repeatedly shows you it cannot or will not handle that. "I realized not everyone is deserving of that vulnerability," she notes. "It isn't safe to cry around everyone."

As a result, she finds herself relishing spaces with other Black women where she's able to completely drop that façade. "It gives me life to not have to be bubbly, to not have to constantly project energy and positivity," she says. "It's very relieving to just be." It also helps her discern what she's truly experiencing outside of a public persona. "Sometimes, when you're constantly projecting an emotion, you don't know what you feel," she confides. But around other Black women, "I can have different opinions, I can work things out, I can be messy. I can be quiet, loud—but whatever it is, it's just human."

It's such a damning indictment of our culture that legal segregation has been replaced by a system where so many Black people feel the need to psychologically segregate their true selves from a version they (rightfully) feel white spaces will find more palatable. We can use innocuous-sounding terms like *code-switching* to describe this phenomenon, but that doesn't change the fact that it's a little death we charge as the price of entry.

In her Hugo Award–winning book *The Fifth Season*, N. K. Jemisin offers these instructions for a fictional empire, about how to control a subjugated people: "Tell them they can be great someday, like us. Tell them they belong among us, no matter how we treat them. Tell them they must earn the respect which everyone else receives by default. Tell them there is a standard for acceptance; that standard is simply perfection. Kill those who scoff at these contradictions, and tell the rest that the dead deserved annihilation for their weakness and doubt. Then they'll break themselves trying for what they'll never achieve."

The need to suppress tears is particularly vicious because naming and experiencing sorrow is so integral to surviving systems engineered to shatter people's spirits. But force isn't the only way the powerful constrain the potential of crying to undermine violence. Sometimes, tears themselves become the mechanism by which people express and wield social control.

CHAPTER 7

Seeing through Crocodile Tears

Celebrity preacher Joel Osteen, senior pastor at Lakewood Church in Houston, Texas, is famously open about his tears. "I'm a crier, y'all," he often says bluntly. It's a surprising quality for someone who famously preaches a prosperity gospel, which proclaims God will reward your positive thinking and your ability to push anxiety, fear, and sorrow out of your spiritual life. In one sermon, "Empty Out the Negative," he advises, "Don't go around filled with self-pity; that will poison your life." When he breaks out the waterworks, it's often to emphasize the favor and blessing that God has bestowed on him.

From the pulpit Osteen tells an elaborate story about how it didn't look like Lakewood would be able to purchase the massive city complex they wanted, only to be saved at the eleventh hour. As he recounts a city council member changing his vote, he begins to sob. "Let me tell you, God has the right people lined up for you to put in a phone call right when you need it." As the crowd applauds, he stops speaking and simply cries for about thirty seconds. "I'm a crybaby, y'all," he concludes.

Yet Osteen was dry-eyed when he spoke with CBS *This Morning* after his church was roundly condemned for not opening their doors to people fleeing their homes during Hurricane Harvey and then lying about it. (Osteen said the church was inaccessible due to rising floodwaters, a claim shown to be shaky by people who posted pictures of their rather dry parking lot.)

On *60 Minutes,* interviewer Byron Pitts tells Osteen, "There are lots of people in this country, religious people, who consider your theology dangerous." In response Joel Osteen recounts a couple of oblique stories about people whose lives were changed by his ministry. He sobs, "I feel very humbled. . . . I don't even know these people, but God has used me to turn their life around."

Yet when asked by Piers Morgan on CNN if homosexuality is a sin, Osteen is calm and collected. "The Scripture shows that it's a sin," he replies, "and God can give us grace to change. We've seen people break addictions."

These are strange dichotomies: profuse weeping for how God blessed his church with a sports complex, and the televangelist grin about people escaping floodwaters. Tears for the ways he's been able to improve people's lives, yet casual disregard for queer people's humanity.

But if Osteen's crying might seem somewhat innocuous, other bouts of performative weeping are manifestly dangerous. On May 25, 2020, birdwatcher Christian Cooper wanted to see some birds in the Ramble, a woodland area of Central Park. People who live in New York City deserve every moment of peace they can find. Instead, he got a front-row seat to a white woman performing racist-panic opera.

After Cooper calmly asked Amy Cooper (no relation) to leash her dog in accordance with Central Park rules, she angrily yelled, "I'm calling the cops! I'm going to tell them there's an African

American man threatening my life!" On the now-viral video, she rings the police on her cell phone and flatly says, "I'm in the Ramble, and there is a man—African American—he has a bicycle helmet. He is recording me and threatening me and my dog."

When the police somehow fail to react to her news—of a Black man who may be biking in the park—she ratchets up her intensity. "There is an African American man," she says, forming each word distinctly (in case you missed it the first time). "He is recording me and threatening myself and my dog." Christian Cooper keeps quietly filming.

Finally, Amy Cooper is crying and screaming. "I am being threatened by a man in the Ramble! Please send the cops immediately!" Her voice begins to break: "I'm in Central Park." The video quality isn't good enough to see if her cheeks are stained with tears. But if an officer had been there to hear her lies and see her performance, you know they would be.

Up to this point in the book, I've mostly characterized tears as an unequivocable good. We have focused on their power—in literature, physiology, spirituality, and culture—largely through the lens of grief. But Joel Osteen and Amy Cooper exist on a spectrum of weeping that shows how tears can harm and deceive. It's a truth anyone who discusses crying must grapple with: sometimes people cry for self-gain or even as a means to harm others. And if we don't confront the sad reality of tears cried to manipulate or deceive or harm, we will never understand why many people also regard crying with suspicion.

Clearly, Amy Cooper and Joel Osteen are radically different. Cooper's tears directly threatened another person, as she openly and knowingly invoked the sordid legacy of American racism. Osteen, by comparison, cries to communicate and bond with his audience, to showcase his own "humility" and create a vulnerable atmosphere. But their aggressive vulnerability is united by one crucial factor: it is grounded in a lie.

I don't know either of them, and I don't know what's in their hearts. So I'm not trying to say that they don't deeply feel the emotions that made them weep. They may, they may not, and no one but Amy and Joel will ever know. What I *am* saying is that their weeping is so steeped in unjust systems that, regardless of whether it's sincerely felt, it obfuscates truth instead of communicating it.

For Joel Osteen, the lie is that professed humility. He proclaims to follow a savior who, when asked the secret to eternal life, answered, "Sell all your possessions and give the money to the poor." Yet Osteen hoards an estimated $100 million. Most ministers don't enact those words of Jesus in any literal sense (I'm writing these words on a laptop I own); yet the magnitude of Osteen's wealth enters a wholly different realm of hypocrisy. And it certainly dispels the "humble servant of God" illusion his tears attempt to conjure.

It's a humility Osteen tries to manufacture even when asked directly about that staggering wealth. Oprah Winfrey asks him in one interview if he makes any apologies for his riches. He responds, "I really don't, Oprah. We just feel like this is God's blessings. . . . I don't think there's anything wrong with having a nice place to live or being blessed." He sounds gracious about and grateful for the modest comforts a prosperity gospel provides. "Money should never be the focus of your life," he concludes, from his 17,000-square-foot mansion.

Osteen's tears are a means of shrouding this opulence, of cloaking power in vulnerability's guise. And it's doubly sick to cry in order to get actual, working-class people to donate significant sums to your ministry on the promise that whatever they give will be returned to them tenfold. The prosperity gospel lifts up charlatans like Osteen as proof that God will bless ordinary people if we're faithful, but it hides the way that such wealth is a form of predation. The tears are an integral part of that ruse, evidence of the gentleness he claims God is rewarding.

Osteen uses his tears to mask the inherent cruelty of preaching that condemns LGBTQIA+ people and that tells poor folks they are poor because they haven't been faithful enough to receive God's blessing. This kind of hatred masquerading as love should be condemned as antithetical to the gospel. And yet Osteen has developed a reputation for being kind and tenderhearted in no small part because of opportunistic crying. In this regard, he falls very much in line with a sick American tradition: powerful people using tears to exert their will for grievous harm.

And it is into this sinister energy that white women throughout American history, including Amy Cooper, have often tapped.

During my first year in seminary, there was a community-wide gathering to talk about racism on campus. In the course of the discussion, someone brought up the way some white students disrespected Black professors; one student in particular was named as someone who clearly did not offer the proper deference. In response, she called another classmate the n-word. Obviously, there was an uproar. However, instead of confronting her own racist reaction to her colleagues' criticism, she began to weep—accusing the other students of ganging up on her. All of a sudden she centered a conversation about systemic issues on campus around an emotional reaction to her own complicity.

In a country where tearful lies have provoked murders and massacres, these events were commonplace by comparison. But the quotidian nature of this exchange is very much the point. Racism isn't just extreme and heinous acts, it's also the everyday interactions that prioritize white feelings above nonwhite folks' well-being. The white fragility on display in this community discussion tills the soil in which more pernicious forms of white supremacy fester.

In her essay collection *White Tears/Brown Scars*, author Ruby Hamad notes that white women's distress about race "may well feel genuine, but it is neither legitimate nor innocent. Rather than denoting weakness . . . it signals power." This power is always conditional, she observes. The characterization of white women as soft and sentimental was an innate part of subordinating them beneath white men. Men, in turn, were characterized by objectivity and reason, leaving them free "to carry on the important work of intellectual endeavors and empire building." And yet that same stereotyped vulnerability, when wielded against nonwhite people, becomes a means to control and dominate.

In twentieth-century colonial Rhodesia, Hamad recounts, the power of that distress was so potent that it did not need to be paired with even a semblance of actual harm to carry devastating consequences. In one instance, a man named Kuchi accidentally clipped the rear tire of an unnamed white woman's bicycle. Fearing a predictably racist response, he fled. Despite this wholly innocuous sequence of events, she claimed she was sure he was planning to sexually assault her. The colonial legal system agreed and voted to convict. The very fact that the woman imagined that "Kuchi must have wanted to rape her was enough to condemn him to a decade of hard labor." In the United States, this heinous dynamic is famously embodied by Carolyn Bryant, the white woman whose lies about how fourteen-year-old Emmett Till grabbed her provoked his brutal lynching—a crime for which no one was ever charged.

This ability to wield imagined peril as a cudgel is particularly vicious in a country where racism causes many white people to feel endangered by people of color's entirely innocuous behavior. When I first moved to Brooklyn, we lived in a lovely Flatbush neighborhood. Our neighbors were my favorite in more than a decade living in New York City. But that didn't stop some white friends of ours who visited from remarking about what a "dangerous" area we lived in. Was it the children riding their bicycles on the streets? The elders playing cards on the sidewalk? Centuries of bigotry have conditioned many white folks to register the very presence of Black skin as a threat, which provokes all-too-real physical and emotional responses to fantasized harm.

While lynchings are now a less common consequence of white women's tears (though by no means an eradicated one), that same ability to exert dominance wields power in myriad arenas. In her article "About the Weary Weaponizing of White Women's Tears," author Luvvie Ajayi Jones compiles a wide array of crowdsourced experiences. Asked about times they were victimized by aggressive vulnerability, one Black woman responded to Jones, "I'm seriously having flashbacks to a co-worker that almost got me fired because I didn't want her petting my afro-puffs; the tears, oh the tears she shed because I told her I wasn't her pet." Another woman who worked for a local magistrate recounted, "One day during an eviction proceeding, the petite, blond woman who was a property manager burst into tears because she was 'afraid' of the tenant, a black man, after he raised his voice at her. Just a bit. In the courtroom. She had to be led out and brought back into the office with a sheriff's deputy for her 'safety.'"

I don't doubt that both of the women mentioned earnestly felt harmed and threatened. But the absolute lack of threat in both situations underscores why an emotional response itself cannot be used as an exclusive measure of its validity. The fact that someone feels something strongly does not mean that their experience is definitive or authoritative. And crying, particularly as it relates to interpersonal conflict, must never be evaluated apart from broader power dynamics.

White women's tears wield power, to be sure. Except when white men's tears wield more. The limits of this provisional power were made brutally clear during the confirmation hearings for Supreme Court Justice Brett Kavanaugh. During her testimony, Dr. Christine Blasey Ford is visibly emotional, softly shaking as she recalls the details of the attempted rape. "I believed he was going to rape me. I tried to yell for help," she says. "When I did, Brett put his hand over my mouth to stop me from yelling." She begins to cry softly beneath her words, the constrained weeping of someone who knows that they will be characterized as emotional and unreliable if they are "overly demonstrative," but for whom memories are still a source of trauma. "This is what terrified me the most and has had the most lasting impact on my life," she continues in a gentle, quavering voice. "It was hard for me to breathe, and I thought that Brett was accidentally going to kill me." Later, during the questioning, she cries softly as Senator Dianne Feinstein describes Deborah Ramirez's and Judy Sweatnick's reports of their own sexual assaults at the judge's hands.

In contrast, Brett Kavanaugh is practically histrionic. Looking very much the mash-up of Tucker Carlson and a melted candle, he screws up his face, gulping water between wracking sobs. "If every American who drank beer in high school is suddenly presumed guilty of sexual assault, it will be an ugly new place in this country," he warns. He weeps again as he recounts his love of beer, and how he and his friends simply wrote "Renate Alumnus" in their yearbooks, not as a gross innuendo about their classmate Renate Dauphin, but to "express affection." Finally, he truly breaks down as he tells the committee about how his daughters prayed for Dr. Blasey Ford. "Little Liza, all of ten years old," he begins, pausing to collect himself for some heavy breathing, "said to Ashley, 'We should pray for the woman.' That's a lot of wisdom from a ten year old."

Their dueling tears, and the ensuing confirmation, illustrate how the crying of even a white, highly educated woman like Dr. Blasey Ford is still circumscribed by patriarchy. In a different setting, like an office or a park, her tears might hold the ability to shape the world—even if their cause was entirely spurious. However, in the Senate chambers, her distress about a highly credible and well-corroborated memory of attempted rape was summarily cast aside by a powerful man's blubbering.

Tellingly, Brett doesn't cry for himself, but he weeps for other women in his life: his high school classmate, his wife, his ten-year-old daughter. This feigns vulnerability while reinforcing the social order that gives him power over women in the first place. His weepy defensiveness is simply a different expression of dominance.

Like the tears wept by Amy Cooper, these tears, too, are a threat: How dare you tell me I broke the law? How dare you question this appointment to which I am entitled? But power rewards itself: Brett's tears tacitly defended a system that grants boys and men the right to do as they please—one that still sees women as property. In return, he can enforce those values from the nation's highest court for the rest of his life.

Time and again, white men's crying is treated as a definitive account of what happened while other people's documented harm is rejected as irrelevant. When Kyle Rittenhouse took the stand in Wisconsin—to explain why he had traveled across state lines with a rife and killed two people who were protesting the murder of Jacob Blake by Wisconsin police—the nation witnessed the grimly sanctifying power of those tears. In courtroom video, Rittenhouse begins to describe the circumstances in which he shot Joseph Rosenbaum and Joshua Ziminski, but almost immediately devolves into great, wracking huffs. "I was cornered," he explains, before seemingly losing the capacity for speech altogether. Sputtering and heaving, he ceases to talk, as if to underscore the horror of a moment that necessitated his violence. As he sobs, he turns toward the judge, who honors this performance by offering Kyle a recess to recover. "Just relax for a minute, sir," he tells the man who is in the middle of justifying his killing.

It was a pivotal moment in a trial that ended with Rittenhouse acquitted of all charges. It was also a primer in how tears can be wielded for exoneration in a legal system that has, for centuries, permitted white men's violence to defend white property. Rittenhouse's overwhelming emotion—his professed fear—becomes the only fact that matters. It's no longer significant that he packed an AR-15 in Antioch, Illinois, to patrol the streets of a city in another state. Eyewitness accounts that described Rittenhouse picking fights with protesters aren't relevant, either. Nor are the two people who will never be able to tell us their experience in the moment before they were shot. All is washed away by the tears Rittenhouse wept describing his fear. It is the same fear that let George Zimmerman murder Trayvon Martin without consequence. Curiously, like Kavanaugh, after the threat of consequences disappears, so too do the tears. They've been conspicuously absent in Rittenhouse's subsequent appearances on the white nationalist speaking circuit.

This carefully constructed artifice of vulnerability is as old as the nation itself. American exceptionalism has always swung wildly between an innate conviction in Anglo-Saxon people as a superior race and the fragility of that racial purity in the face of "outside threats." Tears become another way to wield power, the final recourse when all other justifications for violence have failed. When the threshold for your own innocence is simply, "Did you experience fear?" whiteness claims and collects its exoneration in saline.

All of this places crying in a fraught and dangerous cultural context, one that instills suspicion in the motivations that lurk behind other people's tears. As we grow older and accumulate more experiences in which tears cover up the truth instead of illuminating it, we become less and less likely to believe that the next tears we see are genuine.

And it's not just high-profile examples like Amy Cooper, Joel Osteen, Brett Kavanaugh, or Kyle Rittenhouse. If that were the extent of tearful deception, it would probably be easier to mentally sequester these egregious abuses. Unfortunately, tears are used to deceive in mundane ways as well.

I'll never forget the first time I got scammed. I was a child, vacationing with my family in Costa Rica. On the street, someone who looked like another tourist stopped my father and told him an elaborate story about how he had gotten separated from his group, didn't have a wallet, and needed cab fare to get back to his hotel. He seemed visibly distraught in his plea, asking where we were staying and assuring that he'd drop money by the front desk as soon as he was reunited with his things. My dad was skeptical—for reasons I didn't yet understand—and I was appalled by his skepticism. I begged my father to help the man and give him money, and my dad—now trapped in a truly unwinnable situation—complied and lent him the cab fare. The man was delighted and overwhelmingly grateful, swearing again and again that he would return the money that evening.

Evening came and went, as did the following morning, but no money appeared. My first instinct was confusion—I genuinely wondered if the man was okay, worried that something had happened to him on the way back to his hotel. My parents then had to explain to me that this is, unfortunately, a not-uncommon con. They described how people can wield your empathy against you. Even now, with the benefit of a couple decades' wisdom and much more experience with various street hustles, I still desperately want to believe that he really did need cab fare to get back to his room. I hope, even though I know it's likely not true, that he simply got busy or forgot to return the money. Believing his unlikely story feels better than living in a world where he exploited my empathy.

More recently, I gave money to a man in my neighborhood in Washington Heights. He was crying; he told me his wife was in treatment at Columbia Presbyterian Hospital, that he had lost his wallet, and that he needed money to get back to his kids at home. Even though my gut screamed that he was lying, I gave him the money. The alternative was to let some part of me die.

We are born believing that other people are basically good; that they will offer help to us if we need it; that we are responsible for tending their pain if we are able. It's why young children, if their parent leaves the room, will turn to a random adult for comfort if they fall. It's why they become upset when they see another child crying at the playground even if they do not know them. Slowly the world tries to strangle these beautiful instincts. We learn not all people can be trusted, and that others will use tears to lie and deceive. But I believe we still have a choice about whether we let the child within us wither. It becomes an awfully cold world when they are gone.

Crying as a means to manipulate provokes a particular kind of anger. It's an acute violation: it preys on our natural and healthy instinct to try to make things right when we see someone in pain. If we subsequently learn that those tears were an artifice, we feel duped and played. This in turn leads to its own spiral of sadness. We long to live in a world where we can reliably place our faith in others' goodness, and we mourn that we cannot.

So what do we do with this mess? When weeping is wielded to protect unjust power, the tears cocoon and protect white supremacy, patriarchy, and other systemic sins that must be uprooted. And it's not enough to ask, "Is this crying heartfelt?," because, as noted earlier, these insidious evils quite often provoke genuine tears among people they enthrall. This leaves many folks deeply suspicious of crying, and for entirely understandable reasons. Holding someone's tears requires our emotional labor, and the more we are burned by people who misuse our innate proclivity for empathy, the less likely we are to offer that labor again.

Unfortunately, this kind of defensive crying is likely to increase as we make the changes desperately needed to foster justice. There's wisdom in the often-used meme "when you're accustomed to privilege, equality feels like oppression"; when people *feel* oppressed, they often cry. It's one of the reasons that we need structural legislation to repair these festering wounds. If we spend our time convincing one obscenely rich person to redistribute the billions they've reaped through exploiting their employees, we might easily get caught in the web of their own sentimentality. If, however, we simply pass a tax to redistribute the wealth of *every* billionaire, we minimize the need to hear from all of them individually about the cruelty of allowing them to possess only hundreds of millions of dollars.

This work becomes thornier when we consider an issue like reparations—which, beyond sweeping legislative changes, also depends on millions of white people's collective buy-in to be truly successful. Beloved community requires an intimacy that isn't possible if we write off people's emotional responses to the new world we're trying to build. This doesn't mean we must *center and prioritize* those emotions. Yet if we don't provide any avenue to process them, new forms of solidarity won't receive the fertile ground they need to flourish.

Crucially, though, it isn't the tears of the powerful themselves that are the problem. In fact, they represent some of the deepest hope that folks bewitched into oppressing others in the name of freedom can change. I brought up Chuck Schumer and Barack Obama in the chapter on masculinity and crying, but there's another male politician who is even better known for crying— yet with a more complicated legacy. Former House Speaker John Boehner was renowned for his proclivity to weep—a tendency often brought up by his detractors, liberal and conservative alike. He cried when defending the No Child Left Behind Act, he cried when he was sworn in as speaker, and he cried when meeting the pope. In a 2013 POLITICO feature, "Why Does John Boehner Cry So Much?" author Steven Berglas is blunt: "A psychologically healthy adult must learn to deal with distressing situations professionally: If and when crying is inappropriate, you don't cry."

Berglas attributes Boehner's tears to insufficient self-esteem and to narcissism, a take that seems as speculative as it is uncharitable. It's also terrible politics if our desire is to actually change people and not just wield our words as clubs. Many of John Boehner's values were indeed reprehensible: he did real and significant damage to victims of cruel legislation and to our democratic process. Yet crying is evidence that people can still feel something, even if it's only compassion for themselves. That is the seed we must nourish into compassion for their neighbors.

Decades of technocratic thinking have left people convinced that the cause of bigotry is first and foremost a lack of information. People are so woefully uneducated, this narrative goes, that they're tricked into prejudice instead of focusing on the folks truly responsible for their suffering.

But this is a misconception that badly damages efforts for social change. While political education in this country is woefully deficient, lack of knowledge isn't primarily responsible for present suffering. After all, there are lots of people who don't possess an explicit, intellectualized understanding of our political struggles who are nevertheless deeply invested in movements to overturn them.

The problem isn't poor education; it's an inability or refusal to consider other people as fully human. After all, if you truly see another person's humanity—if you believe they are fundamentally wondrous and beloved—it's very hard to demand jack-booted thugs assault them at our border. It's difficult to advocate that they be paid starvation wages, be locked away indefinitely for minor offenses, or be refused access to the ballot. These are all cruelties reserved for people seen and treated as somewhat less than human—an emotional hangover from the kinds of racist pseudoscience embraced by folks like Thomas Jefferson. People fighting equitable legislation may not intellectually believe that there are different strata of human beings (though many do), but at some level they still cling to that heuristic to understand the world.

If you offer new information to someone who files it into an inherently bigoted understanding of the world, the mind will simply find ways to conform these facts into that distorted perception or to reject them entirely. Storytelling or personal encounter, on the other hand, offers the chance to change those heuristics themselves by unsettling their emotional foundations. When we meet new people, either directly or through a well-told narrative, disregarding them is difficult. When we are confronted with their loves, struggles, and fervent dreams, it's tougher to write them off into vague intellectual categories to justify their mistreatment. For this kind of transformation to take root it must be an emotional encounter. Crying represents a flickering hope that this change is still possible.

For all but the most cynically manufactured tears, crying is a sign that an emotional life still burns—even if it's been warped around destructive ideologies or funneled into solipsism. If someone cries from genuine emotion, it's proof that they still care deeply about something. If we nurture that concern and direct it outward, perhaps we can rewire that love so it extends to all people.

In the moment, attempting to redirect someone to other people's sorrow can be incredibly frustrating. When talking with people about the crisis on our border, for example, I really hate saying things like "Imagine it was *your* children who were alone, seeking asylum." It shouldn't take this kind of emotional hand-holding to convince people that we should provide welcome and shelter for kids who need it. A parent shouldn't have to picture their own kids' faces to know that we have a collective responsibility for every child. But if that's what it takes, I'd rather have that conversation a thousand times over. The alternative—to abandon people and let them actively thwart desperately needed change—while easier, exchanges possible progress for feelings of moral superiority.

And in these kinds of conversations, crying is an invaluable ally. Outside of nakedly calculated weeping, emotional tears signify an intimacy and vulnerability needed for collective metamorphosis. To get a better sense of this relationship, I reached out to writer and media host Dylan Marron, creator of the popular *Conversations with People Who Hate Me* (*CWPWHM*) podcast—and author of a book by the same name. In an age of ideological extremism, where earnest engagement across difference is often treated like betrayal, his project occupies a curiously hopeful space. It began with him messaging people who sent him hateful comments online. ("Youre a moron. Youre the reason this country is dividing itself. . . . Just stop. Plus, being Gay is a sin," one such missive reads.) He'd ask if the person would be willing to have an open conversation about why they had sent their messages. Slowly, it transformed into a project where he now mediates conversations between other folks who have sent and received online hate.

This might sound like dour and self-serious work, but when Dylan's face appears on my computer screen, his demeanor is strikingly whimsical. His voice is lively and animated, and he often gesticulates wildly—and never more so than when he's talking about the potential of conversation to overcome anonymity and animosity. "In this era when our worlds are statistically getting bigger," Marron says, "I think the strange consequence is that our world is feeling smaller and smaller, because the world feels so big that we very naturally retreat to what some call echo chambers, or algorithmic bubbles." While no one can singlehandedly reverse these broad social trends, Marron describes *CWPWHM* as an act of spiritual resistance—a space where, if only for an hour, people can engage outside of the internet scorekeeping that makes genuine connection so difficult.

This kind of intimacy often provokes tears. But those tears fall in a strikingly different environment than an internet forum. Often when we see people crying online, we have found the post because someone we know or follow has already created their own, telling us how to react. And, given algorithms' binary extremism, those instructions are usually either enthusiastic praise or condemnation. Neither is conducive to nuance. "It's easy to pathologize someone's tears when someone is telling you how to pathologize them," Marron says.

It's that spirit of empathy and curiosity that he tries to cultivate on his show. "When someone starts crying on *CWPWHM*, it's so cynical to believe that crying is deceptive. That doesn't negate the fact that sometimes tears are wielded deceptively," Marron says. "But even if they are, even if it's more a performance of crying, there's a reason they're performing. It's helpful to get to the bottom of that."

Tears indicate powerful feeling. They're an opportunity to meet someone where they are and discover common ground. "Empathy is the necessary fuel to get a conversation off the ground," Marron explains. He's quick to point out, however, that this kind of compassion is also a luxury. "Oftentimes, when empathy is extinguished, it's for very understandable reasons," he says. "Either we've tried empathy before and we've been punished for it, or maybe we feel there's one type of person with whom we're continually expected to empathize, and we're like, 'Wait a second; that empathy is not coming back to me.'" But even if shutting off that sensitivity can be a necessary survival mechanism, we also need to confront how it limits our ability to connect.

Ultimately, Marron's project is an experiment in testing the limits of our own empathy. "It's far easier to write people off as our enemies," he says, than to talk to them. And he's certainly not suggesting folks develop relationships with people who are actively trying to harm them. "I'm not advocating that you need to go find the most dangerous person you can think of and empathize with them," he laughs. "But I am saying: push on the walls of your safe space, see how big the square footage is, because I think you'll find it's a lot bigger than you think it is." And in this work, crying is an invaluable ally. It helps open a door we can walk through together, toward a relationship grounded in the humanity that connects us.

The experience of crying with one person—seeing and holding their personhood—invites us to widen that circle. If we can walk with people to the point where we are weeping over neighbors we do not know, it sows the seeds for lasting transformation. Heightened emotional response is a signal to our brains that what we are learning is important. It allows new ideas to stick and creates long-term memories that last well beyond the immediate moment. Evolutionarily, that heightened affect is a signal that this new information might be crucial to survival. And in this moment, it absolutely is. We will not collectively survive if we don't swiftly and radically change. The climate crisis, rising fascism, an epidemic of gun violence, deepening poverty—these horrors and more require immediate action.

The degree culture must shift—and the relatively short window in which we can avert absolute catastrophe—requires more than technocratic tinkering at the edges of society. We need a conversion, like Paul experienced on the road to Damascus. In the book of Acts, the preacher formerly known as Saul begins the story as a murderous official kicking down doors to imprison folks who follow Jesus. Suddenly, however, he is blinded and spends the next few days wandering about, aimless and lost. Finally, as his heart transforms, scales fall from his eyes and he is able to see again. Immediately he begins to proclaim the love he once persecuted.

It's this kind of rebirth that can remake culture. But it requires moral courage that dreams bigger than patching a long-shredded safety net. We must weave a new world from whole cloth and reject those who make a living selling patches they know are insufficient for mending what we've torn. While brilliant flashes of heavenly light may not be forthcoming, the radical transformation that can save us would be no less dramatic. But to turn from systems of brutality and death, tears, not scales, must fall from our eyes.

If crocodile tears represent one extreme of human weeping, we must wholeheartedly commit ourselves to the other. Our hearts must find the current violence intolerable. It should physically and emotionally pain every person when one out of three families with children are food insecure. When mass shootings become so quotidian that they increasingly miss the headlines, our eyes should not be dry. Widespread police murders demand howls of rage and grief. And the cruel selfishness of public servants who politicized pandemic safety precautions—choices that killed hundreds of thousands of people—should ignite a season of weeping that brings government to its knees.

Until this accursed and stifling silence is replaced by widespread lamentation, we will not be able to muster the coalitions we need. Crying is deep religion, in the true etymological sense of the word *religare*, "to bind"; it tethers us to one another, rekindling the love for which we were created. When we weep for one another we profess commitment to our respective lives—and a steadfast courage to build something better together. That's why, as much as the tears described in this chapter are insidious and destructive, we should not write them off entirely. They need to be redirected from the poisonous ideologies that hold them captive and freed to water liberation.

We must learn from communities that embrace prophetic weeping, those who cry hard to bring a softer world near. Queer folks who braid grief and joy into potent action; children who have not yet learned to cry with guile or stifle tears; Black folks whose wails, moans, and triumphant joy fuel resistance: these and more chart a course for the future we deserve. If we sit at their feet, everyone can learn to cry the kinds of tears that make transformation possible.

While I was in seminary, I had the great fortune to sing in a gospel choir that M. Roger Holland II directed. Once, in a chapel service as we were singing "Total Praise," I began to break down. Beneath arching columns, I felt so small and yet wondrously enmeshed with everyone singing beside me. The chorus of that beloved gospel song majestically proclaims our own limits, our need for salvation in a power wider than ourselves: "You are the source of my strength. You are the strength of my life." As I sang, I felt the tears on my lips before I realized I was crying. The words helped me relinquish the delusion I could thrive on my own. It suddenly seemed absurd that anyone should even want to.

Musical inversions are an incredible emotional trick. The various parts rotate, and all of the sudden my tenor line would become the melody. My own voice, on its own a shaking reed in that hall, ducked and swooped between the other parts. The music swelled and those tears broke into wracking sobs—but somehow all without breaking my ability to continue singing those praises. The experience of giving oneself in complete surrender is ecstatic; it's shattering in ways that help you finally feel whole. And wed to liberation theology in the pulpit, it's a call to resurrection that transcends the limits of what we're told is possible.

I was a scared twenty-one-year-old queer kid—still learning to love myself and know that God loved *all* of me. But as the key modulated and rose, I felt my own worth in ways that surpassed any intellectual acceptance. I began to slough off the toxic residue I still carried, abandoning my inheritance from systems never invested in my thriving. And when the song was over that ecstasy lingered, and I loved myself differently and palpably knew God. In the words of the mystic Howard Thurman, "What the world needs is more people who have come alive." Finally I was living. And today weeping just might hold the secret to rescue all of us from the brink of death.

CHAPTER 8

The Queer Art of Crying

I lied a lot in chapters 4 and 5. Okay, perhaps it wasn't lying, per se. But I spent a good ten thousand words talking about crying within a gender binary that, frankly, does not exist.

Gender is a spectrum, and a more complicated one than a simple male-female axis. Many of my nonbinary friends don't view their gender as some metaphysical land in-between masculinity and femininity; rather, they know themselves to be wholly outside those two poles. Even the seemingly stable ends of that spectrum begin to dissolve under closer examination. These days, I'm less and less comfortable calling myself a man because, when asked what, exactly, constitutes my maleness, I don't have satisfactory answers. The gender explanation in which I most often seek refuge comes from Judith Butler's *Gender Trouble*, in which she describes gender as the sum total of our behaviors—a performance we create and recreate throughout our lives. "Gender ought not to be conceived as a noun or a substantial thing or a static cultural marker," she writes, "but rather as an incessant and repeated action."

It's important to talk about how "men" and "women" are socialized differently because, unfortunately, our world does shape people in rigid and damaging ways based on their perceived gender. This process begins well before we take our first breath, as the myriad gender reveal parties that pollute our social media feeds attest. (Truly, the only honest revelations in that perverse party genre are the ones that have started forest fires, because they literally enact the devastating effects wrought by highly gendered cultures.) In analyzing the effects of that socialization, however, we should never forget that it's fundamentally grounded in falsehood.

Shattering the myth of the gender binary doesn't just break constructs that are actively binding people; it frees us to cry more authentically, too. I wrote about gender in a binary for simplicity's sake, but also because it illuminates the cultural forces that complicate people's relationship with crying. The binary gender system, after all, is not an inescapable natural destiny but a political and cultural choice to favor particular outcomes. "There is no reason to divide up human bodies into male and female sexes," Butler writes, "except that such a division suits the economic needs of heterosexuality and lends a naturalistic gloss to the institution of heterosexuality." The cultural restraints we impose on crying are not incidental; they serve to reinforce that institution and support the division of life into public and private spheres—men and women safely ensconced in their respective domains.

Acculturating boys to be tough and unfeeling prepares them to move seamlessly through a professional world where men have made emotional numbness a prerequisite for success. Shaping girls to be emotional and empathetic renders them ill-fit to thrive in public spaces that were never designed for them while simultaneously preparing them to raise children. Much has been written about the performative helplessness men frequently adopt to get out of daily tasks like grocery shopping. ("I can't go; I don't know where anything is!") The historic pruning of men's emotional lives is this gambit but on a much more dramatic scale. By making men cold and unavailable, they are rendered unfit to be primary caregivers, imprisoning women in a role our social systems wish them to fulfill.

So many of the constraints and restrictions we looked at in the previous chapters arise from fears that our tears violate proper gender performance: "Cowboys don't cry," or "If I cry, people won't think I'm capable, and it's already hard enough to be a woman in this office." This entire edifice of raising boys to be men and girls to be women is built upon a foundation that traps *everyone*, not just those of us who fall beyond tidy gender definitions.

Tears are disruptive. They demand their own space and attention. They refuse to let people pretend an unjust order is preferable to a more just chaos, and in that wildness, they carve space for people to be free. Likewise, an understanding of gender that breaks essentialist lies through lived authenticity doesn't just create liberatory space for trans and gender-expansive people; it invites everyone into freedom.

Even in groups of people who fit comfortably within cisgender norms, few feel at home in *all* aspects of stereotypical masculinity or femininity. A cursory Etsy browse reveals cheugy t-shirts proclaiming "F-Bomb Mom: I Sprinkle That Shit Like Confetti," and "I May Be Cute But I'm Also Ferocious," and "Real Men Wear Pink." It's why we have terms like *tomboy* or *metrosexual*—words that celebrate deviance from strict gender performance while simultaneously reinforcing the existence of a "normal" way to be a woman or a man. If more cisgender people understood gender as inherently performative rather than as a fixed, intrinsic quality, we wouldn't spend so much time worrying whether Hillary Clinton's tears were "authentic."

And perhaps I wouldn't have stifled my own from fear they somehow made me less of a man.

When I told you how and why I stopped crying, I didn't mention that it was also an expression of my own internalized homophobia. At the same time that I realized the other boys in my class belittled those who cried, I was also realizing that I found some of them attractive. Like many queer kids, I was stuck between my own burgeoning sexuality and a relatively clear-eyed understanding that living fully and authentically as myself would invite torment and ridicule. So I buried that attraction as deeply as I could, convinced that if I could lie to myself well enough, perhaps I could deceive the world as well.

The problem with crafting a prison within your own shame, however, is that it's a terrifyingly precarious construction. I was habitually afraid that, by the slightest slip, I would reveal my bisexuality to others with a clarity I wasn't even ready to offer myself. I remember in seventh grade being asked to look at my nails. When I stretched out my hand in front of me, fingers spread, the act met with guffaws from boys in my class, who scoffed and told me that was the "gay" way to look at one's fingers. While other kids might have been able to easily shrug off that kind of ridiculous sophomoric joke, for me it ignited full-blown panic. Surely this would be the moment that everyone would know. And not only would they mock me, but I'd have to be honest with myself as well. Frankly, I don't know which I feared more.

Crying has been so thoroughly associated with homosexuality in men that it was an early victim in this self-directed purge. Granted, it's a roundabout association, because clearly there's nothing intrinsically "gay" about emotional lacrimation. But tears *are* linked to weakness in the canon of toxic masculinity, and there's nothing weaker by that estimation than men who "misdirect" our lust and longing. It's a worldview that's still deeply influenced by patriarchal notions of a hierarchy within genders, one that men break if we submit ourselves to other men. (It's why, at various points in history, homosexuality between women was ignored—if not socially permissible—while masculine gayness was vilified. By being penetrated, so the twisted logic goes, a man is no longer fully a man; we are made not into women but something less than what we were.) This category crisis destabilizes the traditional hierarchy, threatening to pull the whole thing down.

By extinguishing my own tears, I was unknowingly participating in that perverse order. I did not know the overarching history, but on an instinctual level I had perceived enough to know that too much open crying might give away my most closely guarded secret. Crying is revelatory. It shows what lurks beneath the surface, and it's a threat to those who wish to keep things buried.

And this is precisely why crying is actually an unequivocal strength, in men or anyone else. Dangerous truths will set us free, but revealing them requires courage. Queerness not only destabilizes ancient social orders designed to cage and imprison; it builds new structures of belonging that prioritize emotional authenticity.

In his book *The Queer Art of Failure*, Jack Halberstam outlines ways that queer culture has thrived precisely by refusing (or being unable) to live by culturally defined goalposts. "What kinds of reward can failure offer us?" he asks. "Perhaps most obviously, failure allows us to escape the punishing norms that discipline behavior and manage human development with the goal of delivering us from unruly childhoods to orderly and predictable adulthoods." Crying, and other signs of "failure," Halberstam writes, "preserve some of the wondrous anarchy of childhood and disturb the supposedly clean boundaries between adults and children, winners and losers."

In his book, Halberstam offers a chaotic romp through queer art and "low" culture—the book opens with an extended analysis of Spongebob Squarepants and includes a beautiful chapter examining the virtues of forgetting as extolled by *Dude, Where's My Car*—and he outlines how queer rejection of social norms charts new horizons for joy and freedom. Since these cultural rules were erected for us to fail (and, frankly, also harm the folks who are able to follow them), the only true liberation comes through embracing that failure. Halberstam is careful and right to point out that embracing failure is not a victory without its own inherent pain, but he powerfully captures the beauty of living within that loss.

These dynamics of "failure" play out within the punishing contours of capitalist and heteronormative society. When stable and even lucrative employment is necessary to provide basic necessities like shelter and healthcare, in a country that still habitually discriminates against queer folks in the workplace, failure ought to be debilitating. Likewise, when social capital often hinges on willingness to marry and dutifully produce two and a half children, the shadows of this mandatory domestic bliss could be devastating. And yet queer communities are filled with folks who not only endure this cultural harm but thrive in its wake.

A huge source of this resilience is the willingness to live an emotionally authentic life. If we can be present, even in pain, it magnifies our jubilation. This beautiful alchemy can transform tears of sorrow or shame into joyful, ecstatic release. There's a reason exuberant dancing will always make a home in queer communities. Even in the shadow of death, queer folks have found and will always find new life. It's a dynamic that Halberstam sees exemplified in the animated film *Chicken Run*. Rather than head docilely to their eventual slaughter, the chickens choose utopian community. "The lead chicken, Ginger, proposes to her sisterhood that there must be more to life than sitting around and producing eggs for the Tweedys or not producing eggs and ending up on the chopping block." She beckons her sisters to pursue an anarchic revolution that cannot promise safety but that preserves hope for an authentic life. I'd rather cry because I've been harmed by oppressive systems than weep because I've surrendered myself to them.

The refusal to adopt toxic dynamics under the guise of "normalcy" extends beyond individual relationships with "success." Queer people—by dint of the way our innate longing transgresses cultural boundaries—have long formed interpersonal partnership in ways that both violate accepted norms *and* create healthier relationships. And the sexual freedom that queer people have found in one another's arms is integrally tied to the ongoing fight for political freedom. For a very long time, there were no established scripts for LGBTQIA+ relationships—and the scripts that now exist are very fresh, ink still drying on the page. Because our deepest desires are already taboo, there's less compunction to follow heteronormative patterns. The first time I slept with a man in college, that feeling of liberation was intoxicating—a freedom to chart a new course between the two of us. And while it can certainly be frightening or confusing, it's an opportunity to negotiate relationships from a cleaner slate to create a coupling that truly serves both people. Even when I was unready to publicly come out, I felt rapturous joy crying as I affirmed such a long-buried part of myself. And even though the man I was sleeping with wished I had the courage to be more open, and told me so, his gentleness in holding my journey exemplified the tenderness all people deserve. This process of deep consent is a gift LGBTQIA+ people can bestow on broader culture, if folks would only listen.

But liberatory or ecstatic tears are surely not the only one queer folks shed. No amount of euphoric, interpersonal joy can exorcise the ongoing violence wielded against queer communities. Yet the tears LGBTQIA+ people have wept *amid* that violence have helped folks live in defiance of its grip.

I'm too young to know or remember the AIDS crisis, other than the stories I've been handed, but I know what it's like to grow up in a house beside a ghost. My parents' best friend Paul died from AIDS when I was a baby. There are photos of me happily playing piano on his lap . . . and then nothing. I can't count the number of times I've cried at AIDS memorials thinking about him, mourning a future he deserved. It's a particular kind of sorrow to grieve someone you never got to know. I suppose that legacy is part of why I've always felt called to hear stories from older queer folks about what it was like to survive a plague. And it's a reminder that grief and rage are holy. When you're abandoned by the government, family, churches, and all the other institutions that are supposed to hold and protect you, tears become both salve and Molotov cocktail. And God blesses both as holy.

It's easy to forget just how cavalier folks like Ronald Reagan were about mass death—once they discovered who was dying. Indeed, when the Reagan White House was first asked about AIDS,

the immediate reaction was to joke about it. Journalist Lester Kinsolving asked press secretary Larry Speakes, "Does the president
have any reaction to the announcement by the Centers for Disease
Control in Atlanta that AIDS is now an epidemic in over six hundred cases?" When Speakes confessed to knowing nothing about
it, Kinsolving followed up: "Over a third of them have died. It's
known as 'gay plague.'" The response was overwhelming laughter
in the press pool and an incredulous Speakes. "There's been no
personal experience *here*, Larry," he responded. "I don't have it,
do you?" It took Ronald Reagan another three years, and thousands of deaths, before he even mentioned AIDS for the first time.

Two years after *that*, the president made his first comprehensive remarks about the epidemic. When he arrived on a tarmac
in Philadelphia, offered a chance to speak about an illness that
had already killed more than thirteen thousand Americans, his
comforting words were, "I think that abstinence has been lacking
in much of our education. And one of the things that's wrong
about our education is that no values of right and wrong are
being taught." Faced with gaunt people dying in hospital beds,
President Reagan chose to blame them for their illness. And his
actions matched his rhetoric—the bulk of money for federal
AIDS research was apportioned by Congress, against the White
House's recommendations.

There's a particular rage in watching people die while those
with the power to do something idly watch. Grief folds on itself,
doubling back to primal screams. As I spoke with folks who lost
loved ones to AIDS, my mind kept straying to the unnamed narrator of Psalm 137. The Babylonian army has just sacked the city
of Jerusalem, and the remaining citizens are being marched to
forced exile. "By the rivers of Babylon there we sat down and
there we wept when we remembered Zion," the narrator says.

"On the willows there we hung our harps. For there our captors asked us for songs." These are the harrowing words of someone from whom everything has been stolen, someone with a future that promises only more desolation.

Often, when this psalm is read in churches, the reader stops the reading before the final verses: "O daughter Babylon, you devastator! . . . Happy shall they be who take your little ones and dash them against the rock." The anger is too stark and unsettling. It's sorrow stripped of any façade or pretense, just sheer rage toward oppressive power.

In these circumstances, it would be easy and understandable to give oneself fully over to that fury—to let it consume and become you. Yet while anger shines through brightly in AIDS Coalition to Unleash Power (ACT UP) protests, the movement also featured joy and even a morbid humor that enabled folks to keep on fighting. Offered a choice between death and more death, folks found a way to choose life anyway, to cling to love even as it trickled through their hands.

That decision to fight did not, however, mean that people avoided a full encounter with grief. Timothy Santamour participated in ACT UP protests, but only after he had spent years providing end-of-life care for his friends who were dying. "We were crying constantly," he says. "Anything would set you off, at the same time you were taking care of people your friends are also coming to you to say they just tested positive . . . and you knew what that meant for them." And again, that personal grief was compounded by government's complete abandonment. Nursing the dying and even care for the dead was left to folks like Timothy. "We had to put people's bodies in body bags because people wouldn't touch them," he remembers. "It was devastating."

At a certain point, however, the repeated onslaught of unjust grief gives way to a refusal to let more people die. "We were just supposed to sit back and take it," Santamour recalls. "[But] you finally get to the point when the community has had enough, and is going to shift from burying their dead to marching through the streets, trying to reclaim their position in society."

It was precisely the potent mixture of raw grief and rage that lent public actions such prophetic power. On October 11, 1992, some eight thousand people staged a political funeral in Washington, DC, in which they carried the ashes of loved ones who had died from AIDS and scattered them on the White House lawn to indict the administrations that sat and watched them die. "It was a mournful, solemn pace and walk," Santamour remembers. But in addition to publicly mourning their lost loved ones, those in the crowd had to be alert to how police officers might interfere, groaning beneath the weight of both harrowing sorrow and state repression.

But that raw emotion is what set the actions apart. It's one thing to say, "You killed my friend"; it's another to dump all you have left of them at the feet of the powerful. At a time when politicians cast so much shame and stigma on the dying, anguished howls split the silence: *This is not our shame. It is yours.*

These kinds of political funerals became a repeated protest tactic. Like all powerful social actions, they were successful in part because activists forced the system to reveal its inhumanity. When friends bore Tim Baily's body embalmed in a casket, police officers attempted to wrestle the corpse away from those who carried it. What a stark reflection of the administration's central violence: they'd rather cast the dead upon the ground than confront who killed him.

But it would be a mistake to characterize such elaborate containers for grief and anger as solely a response to oppressive and bigoted power. They were also a reaction to the virus itself. The horror of watching vibrant friends and lovers transform into gaunt and haunted shells is overwhelming. Tears and rage name death itself as the enemy. Crying becomes a bodily proclamation: I will not release my love into that eternal grip. The fact that this resistance was often futile does not make it any less beautiful.

And confronting mortality is a blessing that queer resistance offers broader culture. In the United States, many of us have grown increasingly afraid to name or mention death, as if speaking about it clearly might bring the specter closer to our door. Entire industries have arisen to insulate people from its touch. Even bringing the coffin to the grave is often outsourced to professionals. Only a century ago, it was commonplace for friends and families to physically lower the body of their beloved into the earth, carrying them the final leg of their journey. Go back a little bit further and burial was even more personal: people usually died at home, and families often dug the graves themselves. Today, open-casket funerals are becoming rarer, and remarks during those services often focus much more on celebrating life than acknowledging the fact that someone we love has died.

This flight from death has serious ramifications on our ability to fully grieve. Obviously, it's not wrong to celebrate who someone was while they were living. But the more we retreat from naming the fact that they are not living now, the less we are able to find any kind of closure. I don't mean closure in the trite sense of "I was sad but am no longer." What I *do* mean is that if we shy away from confronting loss, unwilling to name the emptiness they've left behind, we are not fully celebrating what that person meant to us. If we do not give ourselves the space to cry and howl, to lay bare the enormity of what death has taken, grief yawns and stretches. Ghosts linger amid the living.

Rachael Ward is a living death doula, who studies the work of death doulas and palliative care nurses, to help LGBTQIA+ people live through death-dealing circumstances. In this work, they name crying as an incredibly important tool to help move grief through folks' bodies. "If we can empower queer and marginalized people to embrace death in a holistic and caring way," they explain, "then perhaps we can engage our emotions that have been, for the most part, disembodied and disfigured because of the trauma we've experienced or the way the world already separates our personhood."

One of the distinct crises Ward sees in folks they work with is how people become alienated from their bodies due to past trauma. "I'm really good at disassociating, and other queer people I talk to—they're really good at it, too," Ward notes. "By disassociating you're remaining disembodied so that you don't hurt as much. Your body floats away and you're not in the room, even though your physical body is still there. That's death. There's a part of you that has to die in order to get through that moment." In this context, crying becomes a way to reorient people with what their body is actually experiencing. Ward is quick to note that this doesn't make it easier: "Crying is a thing we don't want; the salt water that comes out makes palpable the reality around us. Crying is tangible grief." The benefit, however, is how crying affirms painful realities. "It says 'what's happening right now is valid. It's real.' You're allowing it to be okay to not be okay," Ward says. We can't experience resurrection without acknowledging something has died.

It might seem extreme to name trauma as a brush with death, but there's power in naming the ways people are stopped from fully living. Ward offers a concrete example from their own life. "This week my mom has texted me three times about Thanksgiving—and she knows I'm not going home. If I hadn't done all the work I had done with narrative and understanding, I'd be clenching my fists until they're white knuckled, 'Oh, I'll go home.'" However, by owning their history as one in which death is a prerequisite for attendance, they say, "I know this isn't going to change, and I can accept that text and I can break down. I can actually cry now because I can say to myself or out loud to my wife, 'It fucking sucks that I don't have parents who will honor my marriage, who will honor who I am, who will love me entirely.' Everything that I cried about hasn't changed, but I've changed. I feel more alive and less dead than the moment before I cried." Feeling more alive and less dead: it's a potent gift that crying offers.

Some months after I began crying again, I attended a seminary chapel service. I can't remember who preached, or any of the liturgy, but I remember my friend Emily playing the cello. Her graceful notes danced across the Gothic cathedral ceiling, and as I listened, I felt the beauty pooling in my eyes. I blinked and let it tumble. In that instant, I was suddenly struck by the radical transformation of the preceding weeks. I looked up, and my gaze fixed upon a massive wooden cross, bathed in shadow from a nearby pillar. And I felt acutely, in that moment, all the ways we crucify people to make them "strong." The ecstasy I felt listening to that postlude cast my prior deadness in sharp relief, and I began to weep in earnest. My tears no longer fell because of the music's beauty, gorgeous as it was, but through vivid encounter with my own resurrection. Like the disciple Thomas, I had stuck a finger into my old wounds—the ways I hardened my heart—unable to believe what love had wrought.

But LGBTQIA+ people aren't just confronted by moments of psychospiritual death. We also face the immediacy of physical death at rates far outstripping the general population. A 2020 survey found that 40 percent of queer youth seriously considered suicide in the past year; trans folks, particularly Black trans folks, are attacked and killed at significantly higher rates than the general population; and LGBTQIA+ elders are habitually denied housing and services because of their identity. And that doesn't even get into all the folks who have existed for decades, dead to our true selves—even risking losing ourselves altogether—and scared to come alive.

To be queer is travel nearer to death; yet in the face of the enormity of this unjust tragedy, queer people have chosen again and again to live in abundant and exuberant life. We've found a joy that does not cast out weeping but does not diminish itself, either.

Particularly in the decades to come, as climate change promises a series of relentless catastrophes, this ability to live abundantly within our grief is exactly what the world needs. As long as we picture tears and joy as opposite ends of a spectrum, we consign ourselves to live within trauma in an increasingly traumatic world. If we mindfully celebrate the tenderness we feel in each other's arms, however, it preserves our capacity to hold these euphoric moments in tension with the world's pain. That balance fuels our ability to fight for the world we deserve. When we find that power and joy with one another, we create the circumstances to find it again and again.

Queer folks aren't the only people who can learn to synthesize grief and anger into action. I pray this same ethos can migrate into all communities, spurring people into action. While the overarching story of AIDS in the 1980s and 1990s is one in which dominant society, at best, did nothing and at worst actively harmed people who were dying, some cishetero folks found their way into the movement.

Allan Clear was a waiter at the beginning of the AIDS crisis, he tells me, when he saw his colleagues dying. "At one of the restaurants there was a ton of lockers where we could change," he says, "but there was only a few of us waiters. And someone said, 'You know why those lockers are there, why they're locked and we can't get into them? They all belong to staff who have died [from AIDS].'" When you see calamity unfolding, you have a choice: you can act or turn away. Allan decided to act. "Some of my closest friends were living with AIDS . . . and I remember thinking, 'I don't know that I can live with myself if I don't do something.' That was the option: to be either a person who did nothing or show up and do something."

So Allan began attending ACT UP meetings. He was just about the only straight person there, in his memory. At the meetings he experienced that same potent mixture of grief and anger. "It's compounded grief," he recalls. "People die, obviously, but the fact that they didn't have to die—and the fact that they were despised and an outcast class of people when they didn't have to be—they were dehumanized."

Crying can become the physical manifestation of that compound emotion. "It's grief *and* it's anger—one fuels the other," Clear says. "It's a huge part of what those tears mean. It's visceral—it's in your whole body." That kind of intense repeated emotion is not without physical cost. However, he concludes, "The pain of inaction outweighed the pain of action. It's how we channeled our sense of injustice, anger and grief."

And while the rage at protests fills so much of ACT UP's documented history, Clear remembers quieter moments of grief, too. Sometimes, he says, "that moment sneaks up on you, where everything falls apart. That moment for me was at a memorial service, walking into the cathedral and signing the register: that's when it all hit. Knowing I was the first person to speak, I could barely hold it all together in this tremendous outpouring of feelings and emotions that hadn't been there ten minutes before." This chance to quietly weep for a friend cannot be separated from the drive to fight like hell. Grief can render their memory into a revolution.

Queer activism also galvanized a broader coalition with other folks suffering and dying from AIDS, and the people who loved them. Joyce Rivera is the founder and CEO of the St. Ann's Corner for Harm Reduction, a nonprofit organization that provides health resources to drug users. She initially got involved in this work after her brother died from injection-related HIV in 1987. Remembering those early days, she says that there were few resources for folks who contracted HIV from intravenous drug use. But "drug users, their loved ones and advocates, and then gay members of ACT UP were able to create a bridge," she says, which helped develop "greater solidarity, and it was very important leveraging policy to provide access to syringes for people who inject drugs."

Like so many, Rivera's personal grief both fueled her work and connected her to others in the struggle. When her brother died, the pain made her double over. "One night I woke up and I howled to the moon," she says. "I was drowning in a river of tears." She didn't just let that grief stay in her body, though. "I was so angry and so upset, I was prepared to violate every law there was," she recalls. "And I did! I'm very proud I did. I and others, we changed the world." Now however, she thinks that it's too easy to say that grief simply transitioned into anger. "I used to say that anger and rage drove me, but now I understand that love and loss are intertwined. I was angry because I missed him. Angry because he was no longer here."

It's a theme I heard again and again as I interviewed people for this book: the knife's edge between anger and sorrow. As gay public health advocate Donald Grove put it, "We were supposed to channel our grief into rage, and rage into action, but it was the activist community that created a world where I could feel enough to cry." Anger by itself is not sustainable. "I was embarrassed by my grief," Grove says, "but I was a failure at being angry all the time. . . . There was actually a lot of love in ACT UP. It was way more complicated than just anger." Crying helps our grief and anger form a compound emotion. Private tears and public rage both testify to an ability to stay fully present in the face of overwhelming pain.

But there are other dimensions to LGBTQIA+ crying, too, like joy and gratitude in the triumph of living when the world promised you would not.

Michael Roberson followed his chosen family into the Philadelphia house ball scene in the early 1990s. Ballroom is a "social movement and creative collective for LGBT people of color," defined by both breathtaking aesthetic expressions and the creation of alternative kinship structures for folks cast out of both communities of color and white LGBTQIA+ spaces. And while it's enjoyed recent celebration through shows like *RuPaul's Drag Race* and *Pose* (for which Roberson was a creative consultant), he's quick to note that the power of these spaces long predated their public acclaim.

"This thing of embracing joy in spite of pain isn't indicatively ballroom," he explains to me. "It's indicatively Black. It's a Black folk thing. It's an ontology of Black folks in relationship to crisis. Ballroom is an extension of that Black struggle for freedom. When Black marginalized communities are on the brink of extinction, we find creative and joyful ways to survive." For Roberson, that survival isn't just an intellectual assertion; it's deeply personal.

"I became aware that I was a Black gay man—but was not in community—during the AIDS crisis," he says. And this was a deeply painful time to be Black and gay. "They made an intentional decision to allow Black gay men to get infected and die," Roberson says bluntly, and surrounded that decision by "a political and theological justification that if Black gay men were getting AIDS, we deserved it. It was God's way of getting rid of perversion from the Earth. It was our punishment." Sexual awakening in these circumstances carries an eschatological dimension, he explains, when you feel like your destiny is premature death, because of who you are. "When I was younger, I would have intimate conversations with God and I would say, 'God, how could you give me a heart that feels so deeply, and be a person who experiences the kind of hurt and pain that I did?'" he remembers. "I used to cry in silence where no one would see me. I would sit on the couch and rock. Folks would not know or be around; that was my sacred space. It was not a way to release pain but to get God's attention to the fact that I was *in* pain. I could not understand it."

Moving from a personal encounter with the pain and pleasure of his own sexuality to living within ballroom communities changed the character of his tears. "It became a way to relieve grief, water washing over one's body to work through it," he says. "But crying and weeping wasn't just about grief. It was about joy: the Holy Ghost moments where you were so grateful, you couldn't believe that you got through what you got through." That paradox—of ecstatic joy and gratitude in the midst of over-whelming circumstances—testifies to the power of embracing the fullness of what it means to be human against systems designed to dehumanize.

"You create hope," Roberson explains; "that's what a ball is. Ostracized from the physical space of hope that is the Black church, we create our own Black church. It's the cultural produc-tion of joy." Weeping, in these circumstances, becomes its own liturgical rite: a means of claiming and naming one's life as holy. At one event, he remembers, they created intentional space to honor pioneers who birthed the house ball movement, but it's impos-sible to separate that past from the present resurrection it seeded. Put simply, Roberson says, "if not for this community, there could be no me." The moment of celebration, he says, was "an acknowl-edgment that we made it, in spite of everything." The response? "People began to cry." Those tears were a proclamation of what the people gathered had lived through: "The notion that you've been told that you won't live because you're trans and Black, or Black and gay, and you're going to die to AIDS. [When you've] seen a community be on intimate terms with death, people dying over and over and over and over in your face, when you have wit-nessed that—and there was no outcry from larger communities—and you still made it, there's a weeping in that. Not just a weeping for those who are no longer with us, but a weeping that says, 'We are in the land of the living, and we're still here.'"

Like any large and diverse group, queer people are in no way monolithic, and it's more accurate to talk about subcultures than assertively proclaim Truths About LGBTQIA+ People. And yet, if there is a throughline that connects the tears of gender-expansive folks, NYC ballroom houses, ACT UP footsoldiers, living death doulas, and a young man sitting in a seminary pew longing to love himself, it's a commitment to radical authenticity over performing socially assigned roles. You can't shortcut this work, because it can take a lifetime to truly know who we are. But crying offers a tangible confirmation that we're on the right path.

If we are present to our weeping, we know our deepest yearnings. Stripping the façades we erect, we can uncover the core architecture behind all those layers of plaster and paint. Whether that's the gender identity we know in our soul, the potent love we feel for another, or the fervent conviction that no one deserves to die because our culture didn't care enough to save them: raw emotion attunes us to our deepest callings. That honesty is not without a price. It exposes us to the full pain of living, the ever-present possibility that passionate longing may end dashed upon the rocks.

Far too many people have been forced to relearn how to feel—to recover our ability to intuitively discern who we are. That process of reclamation is holy, and I would not exchange it for anything. But it's also time, energy, and effort that we could have spent pursuing our dreams. We cannot be content with healing people who are broken. We must create cultural conditions so that future generations do not grow up in a world that breaks them.

CHAPTER 9

Become Like Children

Anyone who has spent time around a baby knows that tears are the first, most instinctive way we communicate our needs. My partner and I do not want children of our own, but I'm blessed with loved ones' wondrous kids and never cease to marvel at their ability to command a room. I'm writing this chapter while visiting friends and their eleven-month-old son, and I've been making a cursory list of the times I hear him cry. Hungry? Cry. Knock his head? Cry. Frustrated he can't get to sleep? Cry. Crying's adaptation is impressive, no less impressive than his parents' ability to discern the minor differences between different tears to soothe them.

Some of these tears are rightfully replaced by language as we age. It wouldn't be tremendously efficient if I walked into my local café and sobbed on the threshold until someone brought me my latte. Likewise, reading before bed is probably a better way to cope on nights I'm unable to sleep—and significantly less likely to end my marriage. Yet as we replace more and more of our crying with speech and "adult" coping mechanisms, we lose something important: the visceral immediacy of wailing at a world that is not as it should be.

Tears fall somewhere between injunction and supplication. In a way, it turns the famous serenity prayer on its head. Instead of "God, give me the serenity to accept the things I cannot change, the courage to change what I can, and the wisdom to know the difference," crying asks, "God help me refuse to accept that these things cannot be changed." While it is important to accept the limits of our own agency, if resignation is the totality of our relationship to the world, we fall prey to the insidious individualism that infects so much of our culture. We may not be able to personally change something, but we also don't have to simply accept its persistence. Sometimes we need to cry—and cry out—trusting that we can change, through community, what we cannot alter by ourselves.

Children's crying is often precisely that: a call to communal response. As social animals, we evolved in cultures of collective child-rearing. When a child cries, it's a signal to all adults in the area, not just a child's parents, to help. And it's why, when we see or hear other people's children in tears, we often have an instinctive response to care for them. We deserve a world where we can all cry freely and trust those tears will be met with kindness.

It's not just children's willingness to wail that fascinates me, however; it's the total absence of second-guessing, which so often accompanies our adult tears. In the same way that a child will beam with unqualified pride as they take their first steps, they'll also bawl with reckless abandon—and with no reservations about interrupting whatever else is happening. As adults, we learn to ask questions when we are crying: Am I bothering others? Am I taking up too much space? Will people judge me? And while the cumulative effect of a child's tears can no doubt strain caregivers, there's something sweet about that emotional integrity. It's why I find it so shattering to watch children being told *not* to cry.

Now part of caregiving is helping kids understand that they can take a tumble without falling to pieces. So when a child falls and looks up inquisitively at an adult to see if they are, in fact, hurt, encouragement to brush themselves off and keep going is healthy. But that's different than the exhortations not to cry when a child is already bawling. Constructing a healthy emotional container for your kids isn't the same as inculcating fragility.

One time, on the subway, I watched a toddler nearly brain himself on a subway pole. Understandably, he started howling in pain. His father, embarrassed that his family was now the center of attention on a crowded subway car, and in a pyrrhic effort to drain the rivers erupting from his son, half-shouted, "Stop crying! You're fine!" What that child learns, then, is that his pain isn't consequential, and that it's less important than the quiet his cries had broken. Too many of us learn this lesson in a thousand different ways, until we internalize it and begin to judge our own ability to maintain equanimity and calm even in the grips of overwhelming pain.

Tears can be both constructive and disruptive, shaking us from patterns that no longer serve us (or ones that never truly served us at all). When social systems become ossified, they privilege those who already wield power and justify maintaining structures that serve them on the pretext of tradition. I'm not saying that letting your child bawl at a country club will fix the centuries of oppression baked into those walls. But it *is* an act of rebellion against an order that equates good behavior with stultifying whiteness. Particularly for privileged people, refusing to silence your child's tears in genteel spaces can begin to carve room for others.

I use a country club as a visible example, but the social forces that shape that environment are not confined to a squash court. I served a church once that had a special room for crying children outside the main sanctuary. In the pews, laminated cards "kindly" informed parents that crying children disrupted the worshipful atmosphere and invited them to bring crying children into this antechamber. Beyond the obvious inhospitality of treating children (and their parents) as second-class citizens within God's house, those words represented a shocking refusal to create space for God to move in unexpected ways. The same congregation that sang "Spirit of the living God, fall afresh on me" was seemingly terrified that the Holy Spirit might course in ways they did not plan!

This dynamic plays out in a thousand subtler ways, to the cumulative effect of making many parents fear their kids crying in public. I always feel terrible on a plane when a parent profusely apologizes for their crying child—not because I love spending several hours confined beside their wails but because being proximal to children is what it means to be part of society.

How might we move from an attitude that sees other people's children as fundamentally their property (and responsibility to control) to seeing children with a common commitment to our shared future? Lessening the stigma around crying isn't the only change needed to create a healthier environment for children, but it's a good place to begin.

The emotional patterns we develop when we're young persist well into adulthood. Kids who learn to suppress their feelings to placate adults become adults who pass down the same damaging systems. Conversely, children who learn to fully integrate their emotions become adults who create supportive environments in which future generations can grow. Clearly, this pattern isn't set in stone! We all know people who managed to overcome stifling or even traumatic homes to foster better circumstances for others. But it would be great if no one had to start that journey by unlearning damage.

Besides, even with sustained effort, developing new ways of engaging with the world can be devilishly hard. Child psychologists suggest that some tendencies, like attachment styles, remain relatively constant once formed and endure long beyond the circumstances that shaped them. Attachment refers to an overarching disposition by which children and adults form relationships. Some people enjoy what psychologists describe as a secure attachment style: they feel safe exploring new things and taking risks because they have been shaped to believe that they will have the support they need if they're unsuccessful in what they attempt. They're comfortable spending time away from loved ones, because they're confident those people will still be there for them when they return. Other people, however, develop insecure attachment styles: they become anxious, avoidant, or fearful, even when their relationships don't do anything to provoke those responses.

My wife, Erin, has a somewhat anxious attachment style, despite the fact that we enjoy a wonderful relationship of mutual admiration and trust, cultivated and developed across a decade of being together. She tells me that our relationship makes her feel safe. And yet when I go for a car trip by myself, she can become intensely preoccupied with worries that I might get into an accident and die. And she'll not infrequently check in, just to make sure I haven't decided to leave her sometime between breakfast and lunch. Without knowing anything about how she grew up, these might seem like outlandish concerns. It makes more sense, however, when you learn about her childhood.

Erin's parents divorced when she was three, and she was raised by her mother and stepfather, who created a loving and support-ive home. She also spent a fair bit of time with her biological father who had . . . well, fewer textbook parenting techniques. He used to tell her frequently that her mother and stepfather were going to abandon her in the middle of the night. Erin, accord-ingly, remembers hearing a car door slam somewhere in the neighborhood while she was in bed and sprinting down the stairs to make sure that her parents were still in the house. Twenty-five years later, when I leave home, her intellectual knowledge that I'm not going away forever does not eliminate the part of her that learned to distrust people leaving.

Fortunately, many parents do not tell their children that deser-tion is imminent. But attachment is shaped through a variety of less-obvious behaviors that nevertheless leave outsized impres-sions in their wake. And specific to the focus of this book is the fact that caregivers' responses to crying are a critical determinant of their children's eventual attachment style.

Our personalities begin to take shape long before we're able to verbally communicate. Caregivers who would never dream of telling a child "We might suddenly leave you" can still communi-cate that message in a variety of ways. Because crying is literally the first way that babies command response from their environ-ment, the way people respond to those cries is crucial. Babies who are habitually left to cry alone, needs unattended, are sig-nificantly more likely to develop an insecure attachment style than babies who solicit the assistance they require. Sadly, this can create a vicious cycle in which an overwhelmed parent con-tinually ignores their child's incessant crying, which only makes the baby cry harder to garner attention.

It's a delicate balance, however, because in order to develop secure attachment, children must also learn to regulate their own emotions and discover an ability to self-soothe. Parents who instantly leap to help older children at the first indication of distress don't give them the chance to bolster confidence and self-sufficiency. To support secure attachment, caregivers must discern when their child needs care and when they need an opportunity to develop their own competency. But too many people ascribe these dynamics even to infants when, in truth, research suggests the best way adults can aid babies' development is to meet their needs as immediately as possible. The effects are clear early on: by the time a baby is twelve months old researchers can detect clear attachment tendencies. Attachment specialists Omri Gillath, Gery Karantzas, and R. Chris Fraley report that "children who were classified as secure were more likely, than those who were not, to have had caregivers who were sensitively responsive to their child's needs in the year prior."

Letting babies "cry it out" doesn't just cause psychosocial damage; it physiologically alters their developing brains. Dr. Darcia Narvaez is an internationally renowned expert in the neurobiology of moral development and taught psychology for many years at the University of Notre Dame. She expresses horror at the advice many parenting experts give to caregivers. "I get emails all the time from parents who have been advised by sleep training clinics to have a six-week-old child cry themselves to sleep," she says. "Babies are born very immature; they look like fetuses until about eighteen months of age. Every experience they're having is shaping how well the brain is growing. Every second, they're growing thousands of brain connections. So if you leave them to cry, you are increasing cortisol, which is an immobilizing hormone in the brain. It actually not only impairs development; it melts brain connections."

The cumulative effects of this type of damage predispose the child to a host of disordered emotions. "It undermines the baby's trust in themselves, that they can signal what they need and help will come," she explains. "If you don't have that grounding, you're going to always be suspicious of other people, suspicious of your own self. You'll start to suppress your own needs and not even develop your intuitive understanding of who you are." Unfortunately, there's no way to go back and reclaim that crucial developmental period. "When you leave babies to cry, you are now putting them on a lower health trajectory, a lower social-emotional intelligence trajectory," Narvaez observes.

Recovering from early childhood trauma is not impossible, but it requires an incredible amount of work that otherwise wouldn't be necessary. Therapy, meditation, prayer, and spiritual retreats can help us gain a sensitivity and holistic wellness that should have been our birthright. We'll never know the people we might be without those periods of thwarted development, but we can nurture ourselves toward becoming who we would have been if we grew up differently.

Sadly, the effects of neglect in infancy are often exacerbated across subsequent generations. Parents who were raised by people unresponsive to their cries are more likely to ignore their own infants' wails. Indeed, people have an unfortunate tendency to assume that the way they were raised was healthy, because to conclude otherwise prompts critical examination of caregivers they may love as well as their own emotional state. "We have all these people with primal wounds in the United States," Narvaez says—"adults who become parents and treat their children the same way they were treated. The culture of the U.S. is very much against tenderness, and so we're passing on worse and worse parenting."

This situation isn't just the result of intergenerational trauma or lack of awareness of the best way to care for infants. It's also the product of a country that refuses to offer caregivers the structural support they need to prioritize their child's healthy development. The United States' meager guarantee of twelve weeks unpaid leave is an international scandal. Chile offers mothers eighteen weeks of parental leave. In Estonia, parents receive twenty weeks of fully paid leave—and they can then elect to take *sixty-two weeks* of partial pay when that ends, all without risking their jobs. I chose these two countries somewhat at random, but if you ever want to feel truly depressed—or heartened by the possibilities available to us—read about parental leave policies around the world.

Our model forces millions of parents back into the workplace while their children are in a precarious stage of development. So of course practices like sleep training and ignoring babies' tears rocket in popularity as caregivers are forced to choose between what's good for their child and the sleep they need to be competent at their jobs. It's a deeply alienating choice, and one that violates our deepest yearnings. Narvaez explains that evolutionarily, we're hardwired for "nurturing and a maternal gift economy that provides for children's needs without expecting something in return. That's our heritage; that's what leads to our full humanity." Policies that force parents to ask their infants for compromise—keeping quiet so their parents can rest for work—will continue to undermine our collective development until they're eradicated. We don't just need a culture shift; we need systems that facilitate a world where every infant's tears can be held and comforted.

Suppressing children's ability to cry doesn't just stunt their own emotional growth; it predisposes them to disregard other people's pain. When parents order children not to cry it both communicates that their own tears are shameful and reinforces a worldview that treats honoring people's feelings as a sign of weakness.

Growing up ensconced in white Anglo-Saxon Protestant culture, I'm familiar with the pattern. WASP etiquette notoriously encourages people to bottle up feelings and compartmentalize sentiment into deep unspoken recesses. Tears are regarded as such an extravagant excess that they're often absent even in the circumstances where they're most warranted. (Lucille Bluth on *Arrested Development* might say it best: "I wanna cry so bad, but I don't think I can spare the moisture.")

It's tempting to treat WASP sanctions against crying as a cultural curiosity, an incidental habit like croquet or pinochle. But the history of global capitalism, dominated as it has been by white people, suggests something far more insidious. The best way to raise a generation that will maximize profit by disregarding other people's suffering is to help them deaden themselves altogether. (After all, regardless of what might be said about the benefits of Ebenezer Scrooge's change of heart, it's indisputable that he began to spend more money on coal for Bob Cratchit's fire after the ghostly visitation.)

Several generations before my birth, my extended family owned and operated a paper mill in upstate New York. One summer, while exploring the lake house that serves as its only remaining legacy, I found an old DVD containing an interview with my great-uncle, in which he talked about his life as the son of a mill owner. One of the memories he mentioned was his father's insistence that he never go out drinking at the bar in the nearby town. "It's not good to get too close to people who will one day work for you," he explained. These words are a tacit confession of that underlying dynamic. Capitalism is predicated on economic exploitation, and it's much harder to exploit people toward whom you've cultivated empathy.

But WASPs do not have a monopoly on white discomfort with crying. And while the result might look and feel somewhat different depending on the region and history, it's hard not to speculate that this overarching trend is linked to the history of America's caste system. White people still enjoy marked financial privilege from structural racism, and that ill-gotten wealth has often passed down the attendant curse of emotional poverty.

Obviously, trying to teach white people how to feel something when they don't will not mend that material breach. But genuine reparations will not be possible until enough white people feel the weight of that historic harm and join the multiethnic coalition working to repair it.

Part of that work is recognizing that the patterns and structures we have built around crying are carefully constructed. Dominant messages about stifling your tears prepare children to obey unjust laws and systems instead of helping them learn to build a just society. When I talk to Dr. Narvaez about the ways we acculturate older children, she draws a direct connection between suppressing tears and a history of colonization. "Kant expressed what Europeans thought was a good thing: to train children, to punish them so that they obey adults," she elaborates. "And then later, when their reasoning is fully developed, they can choose to follow laws, because you've trained them to submerge their own expressions and their own interests into controlling those passions." This approach does not teach moral development. It instills reflexive obedience to authority.

While this system of education is decidedly counterproductive to fostering loving community, it's incredibly productive to a small group of powerful people. Capitalism functions through a combination of force and eventual submission, and it's far easier to induce people into compliance when you've already shattered their spirits. "Undermine people's development, and you can control them later," Narvaez concludes. "Then you can split them up and get them all hot and bothered about *those* people: 'They are going to get your stuff.' From a brain that's misdeveloped into threat reactivity, because you left them to cry [as babies], you're enhancing those systems that are there to keep you alive. And now you've made them part of people's social personality."

The good news is that it doesn't have to be this way. Parents and caregivers can invite systemic changes by shaping the way future generations relate to each other emotionally.

Amanda Hambrick Ashcraft runs a movement-building platform and Instagram account called Raising Imagination, where she chronicles parenting three children, with a particular focus on how to raise white kids to be antiracist. While part of that work involves overt education about race, it's also essential, she says, to help children navigate their feelings, as that forms the soil in which their politics will grow. "We want to raise our kids so they know that every emotion they have is important, necessary, and right," she says. "That very much includes them knowing that their tears are valued and holy."

If it seems like a stretch to connect honoring tears and uprooting racism, she continues, it's because we're not thinking critically enough about the ways that whiteness functions. "Whiteness doesn't want us to be vulnerable," she explains. "It wants us to have everything figured out, to never be collaborative." She acknowledges that white tears can be violent, particularly when crying seeks to center itself and wield power over others. But, Ashcraft says, there is also a real need for white people to feel deeply and to learn to be vulnerable. "That, in and of itself, is a part of the way we subvert the culture of whiteness."

And while it's important for children to see their caregivers' tears, it's not enough to only model crying for kids. "Where I think a lot of well-meaning parents fall short is having the conversation about crying, to talk about why it's important," she explains. Such a conversation might begin with a parent telling her kids, "Wow I'm so glad that you're here to see me cry at the dinner table. This really hard thing happened to me today at work, and I am so grateful that I can be crying in front of you, because crying is a really healthy and important way to process our emotions. And I would hate to ever hide that from you."

More than anything, she says, this kind of emotional work has to be an ongoing project, because the messages your children receive about the appropriateness of their tears is never just what you offer in the home. "My son Zane came home from school one day when he was three or four," she remembers. "He had fallen on the playground and busted his lip. But then, in his own telling of the story, he emphasized, 'But I didn't cry! I didn't cry!'" She was able to use the moment to have a conversation about how it's okay to show when you're hurt. But the shame that he clearly felt around his tears—despite growing up with caregivers who deliberately go out of their way to praise them—is a sign of just how many external messages kids receive.

This work is made doubly difficult by the fact that the world does not respond to all kids' tears equally. Revs. Zachary and Rebecca Stevens-Walter are a mixed-race couple who think deeply about how to care and nurture children. Rebecca is a specialist in the burgeoning field of children's liberation theology, while Zachary focuses on how collective music making can help kids flourish. They express more ambivalence about encouraging their children to be publicly vulnerable even as they very much share Ashcraft's commitment to nourishing that quality in their two kids. "I'm hugely against shame," Rebecca explains. "I never want my kids to feel ashamed for their emotions, to apologize for what they're feeling." At the same time, she nods in agreement as Zachary explains his fears: "I want them to cultivate the ability to be vulnerable, but I also want to protect them from a world where vulnerability can invite harm."

He says that it's been fascinating to watch how the world reacts to his kids' tears, however, particularly since most people assume they're white. "My parents taught me that crying was not something that we did in public spaces, and I know they did that to protect me," he says. "But as a Black man, it's been really interesting to watch the world interact with kids they code as white, the way they will offer tenderness in ways they never would for me." Still, even knowing that his children will not receive the same response from the world he experienced in childhood, he's wary because he knows that even white-passing kids can experience painful responses to their tears. "How do we teach self-advocacy and true emotional expressions of distress in a social context that minimizes tears, deems them inappropriate, or uses them as a pretext for retribution, even violence?"

It's not enough to raise a new generation with more emotional competence than the broad patterns that shaped previous ones. If we truly face the wonder and blessing of children's tears, it's also a call for us, ourselves, to be transformed.

In the Gospel of Matthew, one of the disciples asks Jesus, "Who is the greatest in the kingdom of heaven?" Surprisingly, Jesus doesn't name any of their forebearers—Abraham, Jacob, Miriam, and not even Solomon or David. Instead, he calls a small child into their midst and says, "Truly I tell you, unless you change and become like children, you will never enter the kingdom of heaven."

It's a shocking answer, in part because in ancient Judea, children were considered little more than property. In that agrarian culture, children were assets: an extra pair of hands for labor, but not truly seen as full people. That's not to say children weren't loved or valued. But that value had a decided utilitarian bent. As historian Shawn Flynn writes, "In the domestic sphere children gained value as they . . . became contributing members" of the household economy.

Some scholars theorize that this was partly due to the incredibly high rates of infant and child mortality. Evidence suggests that until the development of modern medicine, roughly 25 percent of infants died within the first year of life, and 50 percent of children did not live to see adulthood. Families had staggering numbers of children, in part, to offset premature death. While this makes a perverse kind of sense, it doesn't foster circumstances in which parents would be encouraged to form strong emotional attachments with their kids. Modernity has granted us childhood, as a concept, in a way that would have been hard for the ancients to understand.

So when Jesus brings the child forward and says, "Unless you change and become like children," it carries none of the modern "Awwww, aren't children cute!" sensibility. It's a radical, subversive statement about the way that divine will inverts earthly power. In the Roman system, archaeologist Véronique Dasen writes, "education also consisted in training children to restrain their alert but unstable nature, dominated by emotions"; it's the reason ancient carvings feature hilariously taciturn little faces. The Roman ideal was that all the chaos of childhood would be brought under firm and rational control. Tears and disorder were a sign of weakness, an inability to control one's inner tempest. But Jesus, when asked to identify the greatest in the kingdom of heaven, replies that the disciples should emulate the "weakness" of a child. It's an understanding at the heart of his very birth: our vulnerability is what makes us glorious.

In the line that immediately follows, Jesus answers, "Whoever becomes humble like this child is the greatest in the kingdom of heaven." It's a statement about inverting power, yes. But you cannot talk about the humility of children without confronting the truth that some of what you are describing is a willingness to surrender to our hearts' demands. That quick tendency to wail, the acute awareness of even mild harm, is the disposition that effects humility. Our road to regaining some of that childhood blessing flows from a willingness to restore sensitivities that were stolen.

I've always been a little skeptical of advice to "reconnect with your inner child," because it seems like a simplistic reduction of the long and often arduous work of healing. Yet recently I've been looking at that reflexive aversion as itself a trauma response—a way to mitigate the discomfort that comes from engaging pain my body still carries. The years of bullying that calcified into a protective shell around my heart, the internalized homophobia that kept me from loving all of me, the fear that I wasn't lovable: I may have silenced these nagging doubts, but that doesn't mean I excised them entirely.

Cultivating tenderness for those wounds isn't a neatly bound process. In my experience, there's no singular moment of catharsis in which the lingering hurt is once and forever healed. And it's certainly painful to unearth memories and previous versions of ourselves that are simpler to ignore. But the gentleness we can muster for ourselves is yoked to what we're able to offer the world. When we let the childlike part of us just bawl, it reorients our disposition toward our neighbor.

And hopefully it will reorient our relationship to the young folks around us as well. Kids are still some of the most marginalized and oppressed people. We carve special legal exemptions for assault when children are the victims (try to spank your boss the next time you disagree and see how well it goes for you). In the pandemic in particular we've repeatedly seen children's own well-being treated as a second-order concern to what is most convenient for adults' schedules. Obviously, these problems are larger and require more systemic solutions than encouraging kids to feel their feels, but most of them fundamentally boil down to our refusal to see and treat kids as full people. Despite whatever progress we may have made from Roman antiquity toward treating individual children as precious, our broader systems still *collectively* treat children as functional property of their parents. While we work to change that situation, one of the best ways we can push against it is to encourage kids to revel in their humanity, to own their emotions and rejoice in the ways their feelings help them communicate their needs and yearnings to the broader world. If that all sounds a little impractical, it's worth considering that a shift toward more deeply honoring children's authentic experiences doesn't just benefit them: we all stand to prosper.

My best friend works as a sailor on massive container ships. He says that one of the biggest rookie mistakes people make when steering them is panicking when they turn the wheel and find that the ship doesn't immediately move. Then they'll overcorrect, pushing the wheel farther and farther to make the boat respond . . . only to discover that when it finally begins to move they've now set into motion a far sharper bank than they desired. All they can do then is watch helplessly as the bow blows by the proper heading. When you're used to driving cars, with immediate feedback, the delay between wheel and motion distorts perception.

Social change is similar. The force required to shift attitudes and habits shaped over generations is massive, and the returns are not immediate. And yet a sustained shift in our bearing can help us turn with results that far outstrip the seemingly modest effort. By encouraging children to cry, we break from our past and open new horizons in how we might relate to one another. We affirm that the experience is a right and proper way to evaluate and react to the world. It honors impact as a crucial datapoint in a culture pathologically obsessed with intent. And it teaches vulnerability and sensitivity as the true measure of what it means to be strong. If we can instill these values in the next generation, it will change the landscape in which all of our other political decisions are grounded.

We can already see inklings of this in the breathless think-pieces about the way Gen Z is upending traditional workplace dynamics. While I'd suggest we still have a long way to go in encouraging people to value their emotional well-being, the rising generation is beginning to live into this in ways that mine did not. And people are shooketh. In a *New York Times* feature hilariously titled, "The 37-Year-Olds Are Afraid of the 23-Year-Olds Who Work for Them," one CEO reports being unsure "how to respond when her Gen Z employees insisted on taking days off for menstrual cramps or mental health." It was as if taking a day to navigate one's depression threatened capitalism's very foundation. In her defense: perhaps it does.

Prioritizing our holistic well-being exposes the idols we've been told to worship, like relentless productivity and myths of progress. It demands tangible action over empty sloganeering about how we're "making the world a better place." If these workers don't experience an organization's commitment to building healthier relationships, they sure as hell won't be content with empty promises that "We're all a family here."

Crucially, instilling new moral guideposts in our children doesn't just set them up for a more integrated life; teaching new values causes *us* to change as well. Adrianne Wright is the CEO of Rosie, a communications firm that uses the power of storytelling to help organizations build empathy and ignite action. Prior to starting her own firm, she worked for a variety of corporations like Venmo and Viacom, but when her daughter was born she began to interrogate the values she was taught so that her child might inherit a different future.

"I am a first-generation American, daughter of immigrants and refugees from the Philippines," she says. "Growing up, my parents generally frowned on crying. The way that they were raised, they were constantly in survival mode, and so there wasn't much time for them to show or process emotion." Vulnerability was treated as a weakness, she says, and strength "was about what you did to push it away." This approach allowed her to thrive in corporate workplaces that eschew sensitivity, but it wasn't the legacy she wanted for her child. And she realized that, if she didn't change, she was going to pass on the same aversion to gentleness that she was given.

"Parenting helped me understand the unconscious bias I carry, what my triggers are, the very deep-seated generational trauma I may have not realized I had until I've heard her cry or scream," Wright says. Now she wants her daughter to know that crying and vulnerability are the very best of what it means to be human. "Our hope is that, as we're doing this, we're strengthening her vulnerability muscle so that when she grows up she's able to pass this on to the next generation, or people within her circles," she says. "The more we create habits of being vulnerable, the more people can embrace their full selves and embrace each other."

As she becomes a better parent, Wright says, that work has had a revolutionary impact on how she understands her own calling. "We live in a system that's designed to isolate us," she says. "So as an organizer and an activist, I'm continually thinking about how we show up in the world, and how vulnerability can really be your most powerful tool to make people feel and bring people closer together—even people who never thought they had anything in common with each other."

If more adults were intentional and honest about how our actions impact the next generation, we would have no choice but to change. As part of the debate about expanding the social safety net, Wisconsin Senator Ron Johnson said something unintentionally revelatory. Asked about whether the government should help make childcare cheaper, he replied, "I've never really felt it was society's responsibility to take care of other people's children." Broken logic aside—after all, what is society if not "other people's children"?—this sentiment neatly sums up why there's such impoverished political response to our children's widespread and desperate pleas for change. If I see a child as simply "someone else's kid," then what does it matter if they're weeping?

And make no mistake: The Kids™ are weeping. Between 2005 and 2017 depression and anxiety disorders increased by 63 percent for young people. That already elevated rate has doubled in the past two years, and you don't have to squint to see why. A generation that grew up with active shooter drills, a global pandemic, and news reports discussing how they wouldn't have a habitable climate in their adult years has significantly different problems than the ones I had when I was little. The signs are all around us. I watched a recent teen movie called *Spontaneous*, where a high-schooler's classmates begin spontaneously combusting and the remaining children are forced to wrestle with survival's attendant grief. When I was in high school, teen movies were about having sex on prom night. We are not the same. And young folks themselves are openly baring their tears for us, if only we would listen.

At the 2018 March for Our Lives, a defiant X Gonzalez took the microphone to describe the aftermath of the Parkland shooting. "For us, long, tearful, chaotic hours in the scorching afternoon sun were spent not knowing," they began. "No one could believe that there were bodies waiting in that building to be identified for over a day." And then they named their classmates who had been murdered. "My friend, Carmen, would never complain to me about piano practice. Alex Shachter would never walk into school with his brother, Ryan." After this litany of the dead, Gonzalez stood quietly and cried at the microphone for six minutes and twenty seconds. In doing so, they dared the nation *not* to see their tears. Years later we have still failed to pass any kind of meaningful gun legislation.

Speaking at the 2019 United Nations Climate Action summit, Greta Thunberg let her grief and rage be similarly stark. "You all come to us young people for hope," she accused the assembled delegates. "How dare you? You have stolen my dreams and my childhood with your empty words, and yet I'm one of the lucky ones." Her voice breaking, she continued: "People are suffering. People are dying. Entire ecosystems are collapsing. We are in the beginning of a mass extinction, and all you can talk about is money and fairy tales of eternal economic growth." Years later, global carbon emissions continue to rise amid climate scientists' increasingly dire warnings.

These tears are the product of hearts that refuse to acquiesce to numbness when confronted by calamity. We must follow our young people's crying precisely *because* they have not yet learned to accept the unacceptable. If we truly felt the horror of the more than two thousand school shootings since 2013, Congresspeople wouldn't stage Christmas cards with their families holding assault rifles. If we actually sat with the fact that more than a million species are threatened with extinction, we wouldn't continue to kick climate legislation down the road as a problem for future generations.

These tears are an invitation to change, to conversion, and to cast off the poisonous numbness we've been offered. The good news is that if we answer this collective call to feel and act, the actions it demands would foster abundant life. This is the paradox at the heart of weeping: embracing our pain is the only way we can overcome it.

CHAPTER 10

Weeping for the World We Deserve

Eighteen months after COVID stopped in-person services—and almost a year after the fire destroyed our sanctuary—Middle Church shut down our 2nd avenue block to worship beside the ashes of our temple. Embracing each other in the shadow of the gaunt, charred skeleton of a building that was once so full of life was surreal. Looking through vacant gaps that used to be stained-glass windows, I thought of the opening words of the book of Lamentations: "How lonely sits the city that once was full of people."

And yet the spirit in the street that morning was, oddly enough, one not of mourning but celebration. Even though the bricks lay scattered, I got to hug people for the first time and experience the jubilation of knowing there are some things that fire can't burn. Radiant songs of praise cascaded from still-masked lips. The mood was so joyful it brought neighbors out from their homes, and we saw people dancing on nearby fire escapes.

I didn't even make it through the sound check, though, before I started bawling. I was a right mess during worship, and frankly, I'm still shocked I pulled myself together enough to offer my prayer. I don't remember what I said. Throughout the service, I would cry and then compose myself—only to dissolve again when my dear friend Madge belted out, "Don't pay no mind to the demons that fill you with fear" from the make-shift stage. Her joy was fireproof and infectious. By the time a middle-school math teacher named Alex sang a stunning rendition of Luther Vandross's "A House Is Not a Home," I had given up the game entirely and was just letting the tears course down my face.

As I cried, I realized my tears were a potent mix of sorrow and joy. It wasn't just the loss of the building that made me weepy. It was the faith of people who had already lost so much and who were now daring to sing joyfully. Madge is a performer—one of the many folks in our congregation for whom the pandemic had decimated normal artistic outlets and incomes. Alex, like all teachers, had scrambled and adapted to the chaos of remote learning and the haphazard response of school systems that were not even close to adequately supported. Then, in the middle of all of that, their place of worship had burned to the ground. Yet here they were, in jubilant beauty.

Dancing won't lay brick, and no song of praise can replace a roof. And yet, in some significant way, they can mend that breach. Resurrection doesn't restore things to exactly as they were before death, but that doesn't mean that it isn't real. The tears I wept that day were inextricably connected to those I cried the morning our sanctuary burned, and all the ones in the intervening months. Yet they were somehow distinct—a moment that made possible a new relationship with the home I had lost, one that cast me toward a still-unknown future with the sure knowledge that the love of our community would sustain us.

At its best, crying forces us to confront our frailty and impermanence while paradoxically affirming our resilience. At the bedside of a dying grandparent, we mourn that all life must end but we embody the love they nurtured—one that transcends the hands that held us. In ending a marriage, we can honor that something has irreparably fractured without suggesting that we, ourselves, are broken. And we can weep together in the ashes of a church to proclaim that resurrection isn't just something that *will* happen; it has already graced us. A wounded heart is still beating in our midst.

There's a Warren Zevon tune he wrote shortly before his death, whose chorus begs, "Don't let us get sick, don't let us get old." It's tender and tragic, a plea for what we cannot have— life and health everlasting—but one that offers gratitude for the next best thing: a chance to live and love together. As inexorably as the leaves enflame themselves and fall, we too will perish. Crying helps us face that honestly, but it reframes that inherent vulnerability as a blessing not a curse. It asks, "How will we embrace *this* moment?"

Crying is medicine for a culture that continues to pretend immortality may yet be just around the corner. The steady march of scientific advancement has extended life and blessedly healed millions who might otherwise die from preventable illness. But the medical industry now scrapes desperately at our final days in frantic attempts to prolong the inevitable. New technologies let us sustain bodies beyond any hope for healing, but at staggering emotional and financial expense.

Meanwhile, for those of us not yet nearing the end of life, the wellness and beauty industries beckon with a thousand ways to purchase bits of immortality in pills, jars, and bottles. Eye cream to forestall a crease or wrinkle. Jade rollers to flatten what's left.

"Vampire facials" that incorporate your own blood in a treatment that hopes to forestall time. Colloidal silver and a thousand other poisons that offer nothing so much as the promise that you're doing *something* to avoid the inevitable decay. Soothing that anxiety is big business: a 3.4-oz jar of La Mer cream—created by inundating kelp with healing sound waves—will run you $530. And, when all that fails, there's always the old standby: a little botulinum toxin for that "good" face paralysis.

I don't mean to insult people who find comfort in these products. Lord knows it's hard enough to be a person, and sometimes we all need a little something to get through. But they're also undeniably symptoms of a culture that refuses to reckon with the grief intrinsic to living, suppressing pain through commodified self-care. And all of this will not change the underlying truth: we are in bodies that will age. Death is our common destiny, and the real question is how we'll love each other in the time we have.

Our desire to forestall aging and death may be rooted in an understanding that, right now, most of us are not living well. We live in capitalist systems that regard our labor through the cold analysis of how much additional profit can be wrung from our bodies. We are intentionally alienated from the earth and one another, because people who feel alone are easier to frighten and control. Our culture reels from myriad bigotries, evils that fester in our laws and common life and poison relationships. Our systems are imploding: voting rights are under deliberate assault, roads and bridges are collapsing, Supreme Court rulings and state laws stealing what autonomy people have over even their bodies. And the specter of an uninhabitable climate lurks behind it all: nearly all young people I know believe our future will be defined by ecological crisis.

Amid this collective decay, people grasp for some semblance of stability. Even if it's just the power to eradicate those fine lines or soothe the skin, the effort provides psychological relief that some small corner of our life can be controlled. Against systems of degradation and death, small comforts should never be mocked, but we delude ourselves if we think that they will attenuate the source of our suffering.

Crying, on its own, will not eradicate this deep pain, but it is an admission that it's there. It's a confession: *yes, I am hurting. And sometimes it hurts more than I feel I can bear.* And it's a proclamation: *we shouldn't have to live like this.* We deserve a world that facilitates our flourishing, designed to nurture life. Any addict knows that the first step to healing is admitting that you have a problem. We cannot heal if we pretend that, with just some minor tinkering, we can find a way to be well. Tears cannot build a better future, but we cannot build a better future without them.

While our collective brokenness may seem obvious, that realization does not necessarily bring us any closer to embodying mourning as a public ethic. Consider our repeated haste to open, and reopen, and reopen during a global pandemic. It was a profoundly surreal experience to live two blocks away from Columbia Presbyterian Hospital, where they were parking refrigerator trucks as makeshift morgues, and to hear governors talk about the grave threat posed by COVID precautions. And if that moment felt absurd, the ensuing cycle of shutdown and opening was nothing short of madness. Every time national cases would dip toward the previous peak, Florida governor Ron DeSantis or another merchant of death would clamor to lift mask mandates.

This simply would not be possible in a country that truly felt and mourned hundreds of thousands of neighbors' deaths. In this time, I developed a perverse habit of picturing politicians uttering these poisonous proclamations over a fresh casket. "We're not going back to closing things," DeSantis intones in my imagination, to the family of the fallen: "We need everyone to be able to go to work." The corpse does not rise to don an apron. This theatre of the absurd would be morbidly comic if it weren't so horrendously lethal.

Where was the public grief? Where was the collective mourning? We briefly shut down commerce to prevent the spread of sickness, but we never closed a day to honor our countless dead. The few government displays of this loss—a sea of white flags to represent each victim—were striking in their devastating magnitude but also their inanimacy. Where was the rending of clothes and the gnashing of teeth? Some one million people deserve more than stifling silence and a fluttering flag.

"I am utterly spent and crushed; I groan because of the tumult of my heart," the psalmist writes. "My heart throbs, my strength fails me; as for the light of my eyes—it has also gone" (Psalm 38:8, 10). This harrowing sorrow filled countless homes, but it was eerily absent from our public life. And the way we papered over that pain with exhortations to normalcy is violence.

I'll never forget overhearing a friend on a work call. Her boss had invited my friend's coworker to share why she would be taking a short vacation. The woman had to unmute herself to explain that her boyfriend had died. She then apologized for anything she had left undone in her grief. When she finished speaking, her boss thanked her and asked in a chipper voice, "Anything else we need to get to today?"

This is the attitude we have collectively wielded across years of other types of unending death. School shootings hardly make the news these days unless the body count is particularly egregious. The wailing of Indigenous communities about an epidemic of missing and murdered Indigenous persons, red palms emblazoned across their faces, yielded little more than a shrug from government. More than 245,000 people die from poverty every year in the United States; our leaders respond, "Anything else we need to get to today?"

It would not be convenient to bitterly weep from each blow of unending calamity, but we will never change unless we repeatedly surface this grief. We must confront the enormity of all this collective trauma, again and again, until we build a world without it. Crying doesn't just help us realize we need to change; it is an integral part of changing. We *should* feel overwhelmed by structural violence, not to the point of numbness but certainly enough that we realize community is our only hope to overcome it.

American individualism is seductive. It's so tempting to believe that, through strength of will and our own ingenuity, we can ignite a revolution. This is foolishness. Acknowledging that is not self-negation or a lack of faith. It's just clear-eyed understanding of the magnitude of our crises and the change we must foster in response. In truth, people in power deliberately inculcate this deluded ethos precisely because it sabotages collective action. Deprogramming depends on repeatedly admitting our own insufficiency—not because we are "bad" but because no single person is enough. Crying is a potent tool in helping that intellectual understanding take up residence in our bodies.

Naming our unspoken grief and cultivating humility are personal processes even if both have social dimensions. Our tears' true power rests in the ways that they connect us to one another and create the circumstances necessary for dramatic transformation. Indeed, one of the mysteries of crying that transcends our own physiology is the way it weaves us together. There's something about watching a person cry that instinctively makes us feel closer to them. Even if it's just a stranger on a train, being present to someone's tears creates a tether between our hearts and the pain in another's. This effect is made even more dramatic when you're weeping too.

I'll never forget taking the subway to work the morning after Donald Trump was elected: people were openly sobbing, handing each other tissues. We didn't speak, but in that moment of common sorrow and terror I felt my city's still-beating heart—the compassion of my neighbors and a foretaste of the fierce resistance that would come.

Our tears weren't signs that we would all be affected equally. As I wept I briefly caught the eye of a hijab-clad woman down the car, saw the streaks staining her own cheeks. Clearly she had more to fear than I did. And yet she offered a quarter-smile and held my gaze. We were scared, but we were not alone. As we broke eye contact, I carried a piece of her with me, and I hope she felt my concern beside her too. Obviously, it's a tiny moment. It didn't prevent the Muslim ban that would become national policy nor any of the legislative violence those tears foretold. But community is the sum of these small interactions, and a culture that weeps together—even and especially with strangers—waters the seeds of a better world.

It's a moment I treasure at protests, when the spirit of a crowd overcomes you and you begin to cry, only to realize there are countless people around you who are likewise undone. In 2018, I gathered with thousands of Poor People's Campaign delegates on the national mall in Washington, DC, as my friend Brittany Ramos DeBarros, whom you met in chapter 5, took the microphone to speak out against our ever-expanding military. While she certainly provided the crowd important information about our immoral federal budget, it was her raw emotion that set her apart from the other speakers. She didn't just bring her richly warranted anger at our own government; she carried her love of the Afghan people. She brought with her the trauma of watching our government bomb weddings, schools, and funerals in the name of peace. I'll never forget her screaming and sobbing, "We begrudge for the poor the pennies we give them to eat and survive, but cheer for the nearly $600 billion we spend annually on defense."

I looked around, feeling the crowd weep with her. An eerie hush had swept across the mall. Brittany's whole body began to shake, but her words would not relent. "From the militarized equipment in which our police forces and federal agencies are clad, to the large percentage of current and former soldiers conditioned for war and then hired to occupy our streets and keep peace: is it any wonder that our neighborhoods are treated like combat zones and our neighbors treated like combatants?"

When I ask her about that speech today she shakes her head. "I didn't know at the time how intensely my body was carrying that pain and rage and grief," she tells me. "I was struggling to keep my knees straight enough to stay up at the podium. By the end of the speech [Poor People's Campaign cochairs] Rev. Barber and Rev. Theoharis were literally holding me up." So the impression I had that day—of sobs tearing her heart wide open—wasn't an illusion. As her own personal trauma and the suffering of the Afghan people coursed through her, those tears reverberated across the thousands assembled. When she finished, shouting,

"We will not be silent anymore!" it was as if an electric charge coursed through the thronging masses. The grief she poured into the microphone overflowed its container, rippling outward from the stage. Without anywhere to go, it bounced and resonated; bodies quaking at the militarized death our taxes bless. If there had been an F-15 around to dismantle bare-handed, I would have torn at it until my fingers bled. Crying with one or two other people creates bonds of solidarity. Crying with fifty thousand is the seeds of revolution.

Communal crying couples the conviction that things are deeply wrong with the potent truth that, between us, we have the love to make them right. Mass tears are an antidote to the poisonous numbness of unending death. They are a rebirth in our ability to feel and a visual affirmation that our neighbors are suffering just as deeply. Evil wants us to believe that we are alone, impotent against its crushing weight. This is a lie. We are deeply connected, yoked by a common humanity that seeks to love and be loved in equal measure. Our tears are testimony that we will not let that love die shattered on the rocks, drained by political vampires who are dead to everything except their own lust for power.

Speaking of political vampires, I think a lot about the aftermath to 9/11: the ways our leaders harvested public grief and pickled it into a twisted, sour thing to fuel an unjust war. I grew up in Westchester, in the shadow of New York City, and I remember all too vividly the overwhelming anguish on that fateful Tuesday morning. I was in sixth grade, and after a few periods of hushed and frightened whispers among the teachers, they called an all-school assembly and told us bluntly that the World Trade Center had been destroyed in a terrorist attack.

This wasn't just headline news; it was personal. Many of my classmates' parents worked in Manhattan, several in the towers themselves. The rest of the school day was canceled, and we were sent to the cafeteria, where kids waited for their parents to call and pick them up. I don't recall if kids were crying, though I have no doubt some were, but I remember the stifling fear and anxiety in that room. One by one, kids heard from their parents, except for the few who would never speak to their mother or father again.

I do remember crying that evening—every adult around me was scared and grieving, yet strangely quiet. In retrospect, I know that they were also in shock, but at the time it just felt like something in my world had ruptured. I didn't have words to describe what was happening, and I was not handed any new ones. No one could say anything that would make our collective circumstances even remotely okay, and so I wept, while my parents watched the incessant replays of the attack on the news downstairs. Alone in my bedroom, my body heaved in wracking sobs, more from being overwhelmed than any particular fear. I wonder now how many children cried with me that night—by themselves but connected in the shared trauma we were unequipped to process, clumsily grasping shards of a former peace we could not restore.

We rightly talk about how the Bush administration used this tragedy as a pretext for launching an unending war, but we skip over the public grief in the weeks between September 11 and when the US launched air strikes in Afghanistan on October 7. Sorrow was thick in the air: tearful prayers in church, tender and tragic exchanges between neighbors in town. It seemed like everything was canceled, from football games to normally scheduled television. We sat in suspended animation, gripped by the pain and anguish of what we lost.

But America does not like to sit with grief. Swiftly, a new kind of unity rose: a grim patriotism united around our government's thirst for vengeance. President Bush, in an address to Congress nine days after the attacks, began to transmute sorrow into the desire for violence. "In our grief and anger we have found our mission and our moment," he promised. "Our war on terror begins with Al Qaeda, but it does not end there. It will not end until every terrorist group of global reach has been found, stopped and defeated." All of a sudden, it seemed as if every neighbor had exchanged their tears for an American flag, as Congress voted near-unanimously to grant the President power to wage war as he wished. Representative Barbara Lee remained the lone, prophetic voice of dissent.

We know and live in the aftermath of those tragic choices, that twisted national alchemy that rendered our sadness into war. But I often wonder how the world would be different if we had spent longer amid our tears. What if we had lingered in that pain and hurt rather than assuming violence could satiate the aching groan? That trauma could have been a call to repentance. We could have reflected on the ways that proxy wars in Afghanistan and Iraq destabilized the region, the deadly wages of our sin. Instead of following Bush as he proclaimed "freedom and fear are at war," we could have examined the way our freedom had been used, time and again, as moral justification for terror that made others fear the skies. We could have asked what circumstances make people seek refuge in violence and owned the ways we contributed to building them. We could have created a department of peace and diplomacy. We got the Department of Homeland Security and the Patriot Act.

Until we learn ways to sit with and process grief without sublimating it through violence, we will repeat this devastating cycle. Our refusal to truly reckon with the gravity of losses from both

9/11 and the coronavirus is perhaps a template for our response the next time tragedy might be successfully weaponized.

There's a single dead tree in the woods beyond my window. It will fall but hasn't yet. For now, it stands like a lone prophet, proclaiming how death moves among the living. There's a still and quiet sadness in watching a woodpecker pick through the remains of what was once verdant and vibrant. And yet, when it falls, the trees will mourn in their own way, transforming death into something wholly new. Saplings will spring along the corpse, the nurse log that will feed these other trees' children.

This morning as I awake and read about wildfires in California, rain gently coats the trees in coastal Maine. Here, on the other side of the nation, it seems the land itself is weeping. Anyone who has driven through or near a forest in flame knows the grief that lingers thick on the air, comingling with smoke. The ominous clouds advance, vanguard for a reckoning we have brought upon ourselves.

To forge a different future, we must attune ourselves to an earth that's grieving. So much cultural energy—and mountains of money—are spent convincing us that something is not, in fact, dying. Avert your eyes from melting glaciers, the siren song calls. Scroll past trees older than Rome that are engulfed in Viking funerals well before their time. If an elder burns alive but cannot scream, does it make a sound?

When we listen to those who vacation in space, they tell us science will save us. "We will suck the carbon from the air," they promise. "We will use mirrors to divert the sun, electricity to sift salt from brackish waters." Crush a test tube upon the altar: this is my body. Eat this and remember me. The blood in your mouth is just evidence our magic is working. We are offered increasingly far-fetched lures of salvation, and swallow because it's still easier than confronting the truth. But as an itinerant preacher once promised, only the truth will free us. We must hold and know death if we wish to live beyond it.

Crying is our confession, the first step on our journey toward repentance. I don't mean repentance as the kind of self-flagellation that sometimes passes for transformation, but in the true sense of turning: reorienting our lives, restructuring the systems that uphold our living. We don't need to move deep in the woods to create a new relationship with the earth.

While I was working in Union Theological Seminary's communications office, Rev. Dr. Cláudio Carvalhaes's class on rituals and climate change held a chapel service for the rest of the student body. Seminarians were encouraged to apologize directly to plants, to atone for the harm we as a human species have caused the natural world. The liturgy drew from Indigenous beliefs that there's a sentience in our nonhuman kin, the conviction that we should relate to them like we do to people. More than a few people cried quietly, sitting within that devastation.

I thought it was beautiful and posted a brief note on Union's Twitter feed, summarizing the worship. Conservative media pounced at the opportunity to bully students confessing to plants. "Absolute theological bankruptcy!" the *Washington Examiner* cried. The *Babylon Bee*, never one to miss an opportunity to pass hatred off as humor, mockingly reported, "Disaster at Union Seminary as Giant, Angry Carnivorous Plant Does Not Accept Students' Apologies." But beneath this contempt lurks an underlying sadness. If we truly named the pain for which we are responsible, it would shatter the illusions of progress we've grown so comfortable worshipping.

I've offhandedly mentioned that I believe crying is prophetic. But that's an oblique statement, so I want to be very clear what I mean. In the Christian tradition to which I belong, prophecy is not about telling the future; it is an injunction in the present. Prophets, biblical and modern alike, serve three core functions: they disrupt violence, they name truth, and they beckon the world toward moral action. Tears can fulfill all these roles. And when it comes to our relationship to the earth, we cannot do this work without them.

I spoke with Potawatomi author Kaitlin Curtice, someone I consider a prophetic voice. Her book *Native* recounts her own journey from the evangelicalism of her youth toward embracing her Indigenous heritage, reconceptualizing how she relates to our common Mother in the process. "As we get older, we start learning lessons of colonization—the land is not someone you interact with, the land is a commodity," she says. "We lose the emotional connection we had to the Earth as a being, as our mother, as a friend."

Crying is an opportunity to reforge those bonds, to feel them in our body and honor the claim they make on our life. The inherent violence of extraction economies depends on us seeing the earth as a resource, because once we know and name trees, rivers, and mountains as kin, it hurts to see their groaning. But without re-entering that relationship, we curtail healing before it starts. "The ways that we're trying to go about climate change, I don't think we're going to get very far until we admit that we actually have a relationship to the earth," Curtice says. "We need to acknowledge our grief and that broken relationship."

And if we're reticent about confronting grief and brokenness, we're even more reluctant to engage in the deep work of repentance. I spoke with one of the foremost experts on that kind of deep accountability and healing, Rabbi Danya Ruttenberg. She is the author of *On Repentance and Repair*, and her work dovetails beautifully with Curtice's to help understand the role crying can play in turning from past violence. "The work of repentance is fully owning the harm that one has caused and doing the work of amends, accountability, and transformation," Rabbi Ruttenberg tells me. Crucially, if we engage this process with the kind of intention and rigor it demands, it requires more from us than a cognitive summation of harm. "You have to *experience* it to get that the other person's humanity is real, and the thing that you did to them impacted them," Ruttenberg says. "That should cause you to get it in a physical and visceral way, and to be in touch with whatever brokenness is inside of you that caused you to make those choices."

Crying, she observes, offers a chance to move that understanding of pain we have caused out of our minds and into our bodies. "It is somatic: getting the stuff that's stuck out of your body, to start to break whatever those things are," she tells me. That's precisely why this kind of transformative grief can feel so overwhelming. But until we let ourselves experience the magnitude of that hurt, we will not be able to understand just how radically we must change to fix it. "[Repentance] is supposed to penetrate you," Ruttenberg says. "It's not just intellectual; it's physical."

When I ask Curtice about what it feels like to develop a personal relationship with the planet, she names exactly this kind of somatic intensity. She tells me about a moment at a retreat in New Mexico. "I was outside and I had this urge to put my hand flat on the dirt and let it overtake me, and it was utterly painful.

The earth told me, 'Here's where I'm at. Here's how much it hurts. I want you to feel it.' I was maybe there for two minutes. But can we even handle more than that?" Feeling that grief is essential if we ever want to transcend it, Curtice says. "Something changes in us when we let ourselves fully cry and connect back."

And the *quality* of our grief is every bit as important as the grief itself. "You can grieve without doing your repentance work," Rabbi Ruttenberg explains. "Grief work can be me-focused: what I have lost, who I am missing, what I am longing for." As long as we are the focus of our tears, we reinforce selfishness—even if it's tender!—instead of transformation. "Repentance work demands a different kind of grief," Ruttenberg says. "You have to grieve the narrative of yourself as the hero." This is almost as painful as confronting hurt that we have caused. "There's some letting go that has to happen to face the reality of who we are and who we have been," she says. If we're going to liberate ourselves and our planet from these selfish paradigms, we need to slough off ways of thinking about the universe that place ourselves at its center.

In her fabulous book *How to Do Nothing*, Jenny Odell offers a corrective to the specter of manifest destiny that still haunts our public life. Deified technological progress, faith that innovation will atone for our sins, the rapid focus on space as a new frontier for colonialism—all of this has roots in the same philosophy that decreed that God established the world as white people's dominion and designated nature as an inexhaustible resource for that pursuit. The opposite of Manifest Destiny, Odell suggests, would be what she calls "manifest dismantling": "a dark-robed woman who is busy undoing all of the damage wrought by Manifest Destiny, cleaning up her mess."

Whether that looks like tearing down dams so rivers can follow their natural patterns, halting oil pipelines, or converting urban streets back into public green space, manifest dismantling means deliberately uprooting ideologies that are pushing us to the brink of annihilation. "Our idea of progress is so bound up with the idea of putting something new in the world that it can feel counterintuitive to equate progress with destruction, removal and remediation," Odell writes, "but this seeming contradiction actually points to a deeper contradiction: of destruction (e.g. of ecosystems) framed as construction. . . . Tearing down a dam is indeed a creative act, one that does put something new in the world, even if it's putting.it back."

If stoicism, determination, and anger are the emotional hallmarks of Manifest Destiny, crying and lamentation are fuel for manifest dismantling. Our tears affirm the violence we have wrought upon the earth and one another and confess our own complicity. But they also tacitly proclaim that we're capable of repairing that breach. We often don't cry when we feel like circumstances are truly hopeless; those days are more likely to induce a sense of numbness. But crying is a sign that we love something so much that we refuse to leave it broken. Our tears connect us emotionally to the world as it might be; it's a foretaste of what our love can build. Our tears are not just a means to create that future, they give us a visceral sense of how it might feel to live better. "If grief can be a doorway to love," writes Potawatomi botanist Robin Wall Kimmerer, "then let us weep for the world we are breaking apart so we can love it back to wholeness again."

We must be honest: crying won't solve climate change, racism, or any other deeply entrenched evil. That might sound odd coming from someone who has spent hundreds of pages talking about how crying can heal us. But even I am not delusional enough to think that getting everyone to weep more would magically fix our cascading crises. I do believe with all my heart, however, that it can help. And sometimes genuine help is what we desperately need, and what's necessary to ignite further change. Tears may not be a panacea, but that doesn't mean they aren't powerful. Tears can serve as a correction to a culture that has wandered badly off course. They can help us wash away the pernicious lies we've layered, masking pain and hurt beneath increasingly toxic veneers. When you restore a crumbling house, you have to strip off the lead paint before applying new coats.

It's a bit of a contradiction. Our eyes blur and our throats catch, and when we cry hard enough, we can temporarily impair our vision and even lose our capacity for coherent speech. Yet the daze and the blur can clarify for us what matters most, and illuminate the idols we've placed between ourselves and our deepest love.

For those who are religiously inclined, tears are often our first and best prayer. When I begin to articulate my prayers in words, my brain gets involved and, try as I might for authenticity, too often my brain is a liar. It regurgitates cultural narratives I've internalized and dresses what I truly desire in palatable language, as if God might judge my naked hope. Crying, however, bares my heart in ways I cannot cover. It forces me to confront the world I long for—and what I must do to bring it closer.

In that moment of tearful communion I feel like Ezekiel, perched at the edge of the valley filled with the bones of my kin. I know intellectually that corpses cannot be raised, that I cannot knit together sinews and tendons that have long since turned to dust, and I am left with the desolation of being surrounded by so much death. Yet in my yearning that they might live, all my objections flee. And it's in that moment that we hear a voice calling: speak to these bones. Dare to proclaim a love that can end this senseless pain and close the widening breach.

When we attune our hearts to *that* voice, the villainous tones of white supremacy and toxic masculinity and alienation become quieter. I start to believe that I am not defined by the worth capitalism assigns me. The murmuring doubts of lingering homophobia abate, I begin to trust in my belovedness. I begin to see the fundamental blessedness of my neighbors and the splendor of a world that's worth saving. That, after all, is one of the biggest lies: the notion that we are beyond redemption, and so the only recourse available is to grab as much as we can in the scant moments left to us.

On an episode of Jon Stewart's podcast, Bryan Stevenson—the founder of the Equal Justice Initiative—shared a story that encapsulates this fragile but resilient hope. As part of EJI's commemoration of the more than 4,500 Black Americans who were lynched between 1877 and 1950, EJI gathered jars of soil from each site of terror to display at the museum. To complete this work, the initiative relied on volunteers to dig up the earth and transport it to EJI's Community Remembrance Project, based at the National Memorial for Peace and Justice in Montgomery.

In Stevenson's retelling, one of these volunteers was a middle-aged Black woman, who traveled to a lynching site to dig up soil to take to the museum. She was nervous when she got there, Stevenson recounts, because the place the lynching had occurred was alongside a dirt road in a remote area. Right as she began to dig, her anxiety was heightened when a white man drove by slowly in a large pickup truck. When he turned his truck around to drive back to where she was kneeling, she became even more scared. The stranger exited his vehicle, walked over, and asked, "What are you doing?" Although the woman considered making up a story about gathering dirt for her garden, something compelled her to answer truthfully. "I'm digging soil because this is where a Black man was lynched in 1937, and I'm going to honor his life," she replied.

The man then pointed to a paper she had on the ground beside her and asked if it described the lynching. When the woman answered that it did, he asked if he could read it. She consented and he began reading the paper while she started digging.

When the man finished reading the article, there was silence. Then he said, haltingly, "Excuse me, Ma'am, but would it be alright if I helped you?" She accepted and offered the man her trowel, but he refused and started tearing into the earth with his hands, scooping great armfuls into the box she was filling. "It blew her away," Stevenson recounts. "She said, 'I had a tear running down my face,' because she just didn't expect it."

When the box was nearly full, she noticed his pace had slowed and she looked over to her digging partner. "She could see that his face was red," Stevenson says. "She could see that his shoulders were shaking, and then she saw a tear running down his face." Surprised, she ceased digging and put a hand on his shoulder to ask if he was okay. "That's when the man said, 'No, no, no. No, I'm not alright.'" Stevenson recalls. "He looked at her and he said, 'I'm just so worried that it was my grandfather that participated in this lynching.'"

Stunned by this revelation, Stevenson says, the woman was silent for a moment. "They both sat there on this roadside weeping about the history, about the pain, about the suffering." The woman then told him that she was headed back to Montgomery to take the soil there. He asked if he could follow her. A shocked Bryan Stevenson watched as they walked toward the museum, carrying this box of soil together.

This unexpected encounter reveals crying's limits but also its incredible promise. Those shared tears cannot resurrect someone who was lynched on that dirt in 1937. They cannot erase a history of racial terror or undo the possibility that the unnamed man's grandfather participated in it. And they certainly don't wash away the systemic racism baked into our nation's institutions and public life. And yet, something in their weeping offers a momentary chance to chart a course beyond the present. If only for the two people who shed them, those tears invite transformation.

Stevenson's story is a snapshot. We don't know how it ends. But I imagine that white man has a different understanding of American racism than he did when he woke that morning. Tears take something cognitive and make it visceral; his wracking sobs place the pain he read about into his own body. And I hope the unnamed woman felt in her own tears the power of her work— the conviction that true justice is still possible. Even if they never saw each other again, I'm sure each of them carry this moment and let it ripple outward in their living.

Because that's what's most important: the actions that follow our tears. Do we revert to previous behavior? To an earlier understanding of who we were, and how we belong in community? Or do our souls ignite with purpose—awake to connection and a new sense of who we are becoming? Inasmuch as there's a determination for the quality of emotional tears, they're measured by their effects: crying can push us inward, toward self-centered rumination or entrenching unhealthy patterns, but it can also bring us closer to our neighbors and nurture relationships. The choice is ours.

In the moment that tears spring into our eyes, that future remains unwritten. Doors open before us, beckoning us to enter. But as we perch upon their threshold, there's a simple truth: we are fully alive—brimming with passion and possibility. Our tears are a reminder: love and beauty surround us, and they are worth fighting for. So cry, baby. Cry like your tears matter, because they do. Cry like they might change you, because they will. Cry with reckless abandon: a better world awaits.

A BLESSING FOR CRYING

Because I'm a pastor, I'll leave you with a benediction:

If you've lost your tears, may you find them again.
Know that you are never beyond redemption
and worthy of full emotional life.
May crying nourish you,
a balm for the wounds you still carry
and a salve on fresh hurt.
As droplets fall, may they water new growth.
And may our collective weeping shape a world
better than the one we inherited.
May we attune ourselves to grief
and hold the places we are broken—repairers of the breach.
May cries long silenced be heard in full,
yeast for our communal rising.
Hold each other fiercely,
not to build a future where every eye is dry
but one where we weep copiously
from the joy and tenderness of living.

ACKNOWLEDGMENTS

First and foremost I'm so grateful to my editor, Valerie Weaver-Zercher, who read an article I wrote about learning to cry and envisioned that a curious book like this might even be possible. Throughout this process, you've helped sharpen and focus my thinking while expanding my horizons. Thank you for believing in this book, for being my midwife in birthing it. And to the entire team at Broadleaf Books: thank you. From a cover design that surprised and delighted from the moment I saw it, to all the unseen machinations that make any book possible: I can't tell you what it means to hold this in my hands. And I'm endlessly humbled by all the people who let me tell their stories in its pages. To everyone who spoke with me—all the folks I could include, and the ones I couldn't—this book is yours too.

Indeed, no book comes into the world solely by its author's will, and I am forever indebted to the teachers who believed in me—who taught me how to write but more importantly how to think. To Cathy Greenwood, who told me in middle school that people would care what I had to say, and who gave me tools to say it well. Look, Mrs. Greenwood: I went public! To my high school English teachers Chandler Lewis and Kathleen Heffron, who challenged me to write better. And to my college mentor Dr. Monica Schneider, without whom the chapter on the physiology of crying would have been very poorly written. Even though I didn't go into psychology, the ways you taught me to read and understand research have enriched my life immeasurably.

But truly, this book began when I entered seminary and began to recover the humanity I had lost. I'm so grateful for the professors who expanded my moral imagination, and who affirmed that our emotional lives are every bit as important and worthy as our intellectual ones. To Drs. Cornel West, Sarah Azaransky, Gary Dorrien, David Carr, Esther Hamori, and the late and dearly beloved Rev. Dr. James H. Cone: you ignited my spirit, and I will never be able to repay that gift.

And I'm so blessed by my colleagues in ministry, who have shown me more authentic ways to live. To Emily, Sam, Zach, Rebecca, and Matt, your courage and kindness have left an indelible mark, that reminds me who I long to be. I'm so grateful to call you friends. To my fellow Middle collars—Natalie, Darrell, and Amanda—it's been an absolute honor to serve beside you. And to Jacqui: your mentorship means more than you can ever know. You have helped me find my voice in ways I'm still discovering. And to all of the Middle community, know I wrote so much of this inspired by you. Your love shapes mine.

I'm profoundly grateful for my queer friends, all the folks who have helped me name and love the parts of myself I hid in shame. And who teach me daily what it means to live with integrity and wild, wondrous joy. To Amira, Sam, Elise, Will, Melissa, Liv, Molly, Grace, Abbey, Tamara, Emily, Katie, Rani, and Alex: you've given me something no one can take away. And to every member of the gardening club extraordinaire—far too multitudinous to name— y'all are everything. Thanks for helping paddle me upriver.

Finally, no list of gratitude would be complete without honoring what I owe my family. Mom and Dad, there simply aren't words that can adequately express how your love and nurture molded me. I'm so thankful for the ways you affirmed and honored my emotional life and encouraged its expression. I never had to hide my tears from you, and I cherish all the ones we've shared. To all my extended family: you are the ones who taught me how to embody care. To Gran: your fervent love for words inspired my own. You taught me how to dream wildly and reject convention; there's no one with whom I'd rather leap from a plane. And to Erik, it was an honor to grow up beside you, and I'm so excited about who we are becoming. Our lives are just beginning to blossom.

Lastly: to Zach and Erin. There is nowhere I can list you here but as family. The family I have chosen. The ones I treasure to live beside, to intimately know and be known. I simply am not sure who I would be without you. Zach, since we ran through the woods as kids on a thousand imaginary adventures, you've given me the courage to slay dragons. And the tender knowledge I'll never fight them alone. Erin, to love you is a gift. I still wake up in disbelief that I get to spend my life with you. My tears of joy are yours forever—a finder's fee to the person who resurrected them. May we spend eternity writing and reading each other's words.

NOTES

CHAPTER 1

Walk the house: The Mountain Goats, "Woke Up New," track 9 on *Get Lonely*, 4AD, 2006.

CHAPTER 2

Crying helps to calm: Lauren M. Bylsma, Asmir Gracanin, and Ad J. J. M. Vingerhoets, "The Neurobiology of Crying," *Medical and Clinical Psychology* 29, no. 1 (2019): 67.

Significantly increased while they were sobbing: Bylsma et al., "Neurobiology of Crying," 68.

We must look at weeping: Charles Darwin, *The Emotional Expression of Man and Animals* (London: John Murray, 1872), 175.

Necessity of crying after bereavement: Ad J. J. M. Vingerhoets and Jan G. M. Scheirs, "Crying and Health," in *Adult Crying: A Biopsychosocial Approach,* ed. Ad J. J. M. Vingerhoets and Randolph R. Cornelius (Hove, UK: Brunner-Routledge, 2001), 227.

Sorrows which find no vent: William H. Frey, *Crying: The Mystery of Tears* (Minneapolis: Winston Press, 1985).

Great difficulty in securing grant funding: All interviews referenced throughout this work, including the conversation with Dr. William Frey, were personal conversations or email communication with the author.

Self-reported data: Ad J. J. M. Vingerhoets et al., "Weeping: Associations with Personality, Coping, and Subjective Health Status," *Personality and Individual Differences* 14 (1993): 185–90.

Seven or eight hours after the fact: Joan Didion, *The Year of Magical Thinking* (New York: Knopf, 2005), 28.

I needed to be alone: Didion, *Year of Magical Thinking*, 33.

NOTES

Tears have contributed: Martijn J. H. Balsters et al., "Emotional Tears Facilitate the Recognition of Sadness and the Perceived Need for Social Support," *Evolutionary Psychology* 11, no. 1 (2013): 149.

Someone else's tears: Balsters et al., "Emotional Tears Facilitate," 156.

Superior to an acoustic signal: Bylsma et al., "Neurobiology of Human Crying," 64.

It increases their viscosity: Heather Christie, *The Crying Book* (New York: Catapult, 2019), 148.

Other animals clearly communicate their needs: Frey, *Crying*, 7.

Researchers in every single country: Janis H. Zickfeld et al., "Tears Evoke the Intention to Offer Social Support: A Systematic Investigation of the Interpersonal Effects of Emotional Crying across 41 Countries," *Journal of Experimental Social Psychology* 95 (2021).

Consider our proclivity to cry: P. Hill and R. B. Martin, "Empathic Weeping, Social Communication, and Cognitive Dissonance," *Journal of Social and Clinical Psychology* 16 (1997): 299–322.

Some of the women: Hans J. Ladegaard, "Crying as Communication in Domestic Helper Narratives: Towards a Social Psychology of Crying in Discourse," *Journal of Language and Social Psychology* 33, no. 6 (December 2014): 599.

Crying is good for the heart: Ladegaard, "Crying as Communication," 599.

No support for the view: Martin & Labott, "Mood Following Emotional Crying: Effects of the Situation," *Journal of Research in Personality* 25, no. 2 (1991): 229; D. L. Kraemer and J. L. Hastrup, "Crying in Natural Settings: Global Estimates, Self-Monitored Frequencies, Depression and Sex Differences in an Undergraduate Population," *Behaviour Research and Therapy* 24 (1986): 371–73.

Strong mood improvement: Asmir Gracanin et al., "Why Crying Does and Sometimes Does Not Seem to Alleviate Mood: A Quasi-experimental Study," *Motivation and Emotion* 39 (2015): 958.

On average: Michael Barthelmas and Johannes Keller, "Adult Emotional Crying: Relations to Personality Traits and Subjective Well-Being," *Personality and Individual Differences* 177 (July 2021): 110790.

Experience disappearance of a barrier: Matthew Pelowski, "Tears and Transformation: Feeling Like Crying as an Indicator of Insightful or 'Aesthetic' Experience with Art," *Frontiers in Psychology* 6, no. 1006 (2015): 2–3.

Protein concentration of emotional tears: Frey, *Crying*, 45.

Frey reported: Frey, *Crying*, 48.

218

Presence of ACTH: Frey, *Crying,* 52.

Levels of cortisol in the saliva: Ad J. J. M. Vingerhoets and C. Kirschbaum, "Crying, Mood and Cortisol," *Psychosomatic Medicine* 59 (1997): 92–93.

CHAPTER 3

I did cry then: Octavia Butler, *Parable of the Talents* (New York: Seven Stories Press, 1998), 179.

Love broke through: From J. Mase III, "Josephine," *The Black Trans Prayer Book* (Lulu.com, 2020). Used by permission of the author.

One tear became White Tara: Taigen Daniel Leighton, *Bodhisattva Archetypes* (New York: Penguin Arkana, 1998), 192.

As she was carrying them: Leighton, *Bodhisattva Archetypes,* 162.

The prophet Muhammad similarly embodies: "The Book on Jana'iz, Chapter 25: What Has Been Related about the Permission for Crying Over the Deceased," Jami` at-Tirmidhi 10, Sunnah.com, https://tinyurl.com /4mtxtysy.

Experienced the revelation of the Quran as personal: "The Tears of Prophet Muhammad 🕋—Yahya Ibrahim," Digital Mimbar, November 30, 2021, YouTube video, 11:49, https://tinyurl.com/4m4ee5dz.

It hurt to remember hope: Torrey Peters, *Detransition, Baby* (New York: Penguin Random House, 2021), 155.

This time it's my turn: Jaye Simpson, "The Ark of the Turtle's Back," in *Love after the End,* ed. Joshua Whitehead (Vancouver, BC: Arsenal Pulp Press, 2020), 68.

Sobs ripple through [her] shoulders: Simpson, "Ark of the Turtle's Back," 70.

The story about a weeping woman: Amy Fuller, "The Wailing Woman," *History Today,* October 31, 2017, https://tinyurl.com/2sjapz5a.

I was thinking of the children: Euripides, *Medea,* trans. Ian Johnston (Arlington, VA: Richer Resources Publications, 2008), lines 1080–90.

Grendel's mother doesn't behave: Maria Dhavana Headley, *Beowulf: A New Translation* (New York: Farrar, Straus and Giroux, 2021), 10–12.

They ask us why we have created them: Jeffrey Jerome Cohen, "Monster Culture (Seven Theses)," in *Monster Theory: Reading Culture* (Minneapolis: University of Minnesota Press, 1996), 20.

CHAPTER 4

The first research to compare tears: William H. Frey, *Crying: The Mystery of Tears* (Minneapolis: Winston Press, 1985).

The first act of violence: bell hooks, *The Will to Change: Men, Masculinity, and Love* (New York: Washington Square Press, 2003), 66.

I don't recall Schumer crying: Sean Hannity, "Dems Gamble with American Lives with Lies about Trump Order," Fox News, January 31, 2017, https://tinyurl.com/35k9p5xh.

The Minority Leader's "tear-jerking" performance: Neil McCabe, "Sen. David Perdue: Chuck Schumer's Tears Worthy of the Screen Actors Guild Awards," Breitbart, February 2, 2017, https://tinyurl.com/3nkpasae.

When the whole wide world feels oh so wrong: From "What Do You Do with the Mad That You Feel?" Reprinted by permission of Fred Rogers Productions.

If we in public television: "May 1, 1969: Fred Rogers Testifies before the Senate Subcommittee on Communications," danieldeibler, February 8, 2015, YouTube video, 6:49, https://tinyurl.com/26b45bt3.

I know how tough it is: "Mr. Rogers—Time to Say Goodbye," RC99 Productions, May 6, 2017, YouTube video, 1:26, https://tinyurl.com/2z49syvz.

CHAPTER 5

I didn't want my picture taken: Sylvia Plath, *The Bell Jar* (New York: Harper Perennial Modern Classics, 2005), 100–101.

A woman's body: C. Tasca, M. Rapetti, M. G. Carta, and B. Fadda, "Women and Hysteria in the History of Mental Health," *Clinical Practice Epidemiological Mental Health* 8 (2012): 110–19.

These weeping bodies: Meghan Henning, "Weeping and Bad Hair: The Bodily Suffering of Early Christian Hell as a Threat to Masculinity," in *Phallacies: Historical Depictions of Disability and Masculinity*, ed. Kathleen M. Brian and James W. Trent Jr. (New York: Oxford University Press, 2017), available at https://tinyurl.com/2s42dd5s, p. 31.

Unable to control their bodies: Rachel Vorona Coate, *Too Much: How Victorian Constraints Still Bind Women Today* (New York: Grand Central Publishing, 2020), ebook, 35.

An entire fashion of "deep mourning" attire: Jocelyn Sears, "19th-Century Mourning Veils Were Made of a Cocktail of Poisons," Racked, March 29, 2018, https://tinyurl.com/bdcupasx.

It takes a lot of self-discipline: Germaine Greer, "For Crying Out Loud!," *Guardian,* January 10, 2008, https://tinyurl.com/mvuwhb7e.

What was moving her so deeply: Maureen Dowd, "Can Hillary Cry Her Way Back to the White House?," *New York Times*, January 9, 2008, https://tinyurl.com/3xnnp2p6.

The US military is an institution: Cecilia Saixue Watt, "'It's Horrible to Watch': US Veterans on Seeing Afghanistan Fall to the Taliban," *Guardian*, August 31, 2021, https://tinyurl.com/yb6euy2u.

I was too emotional: Alice Morby, "Yi-Fei Chen Designs a Gun for Firing Her Tears," Dezeen, November 2, 2016, https://tinyurl.com/ycx3dw67.

In order to properly grieve the dead: Tireni Adebayo, "Meet the African Woman Who Cries for a Living," Kemi Filani News, July 2, 2018, https://tinyurl.com/yc3592mj.

CHAPTER 6

Imminent deadly threat: Erik Ortiz, "Keith Lamont Scott, Fatally Shot by N.C. Cops, Warned Repeatedly to Drop Gun: Chief," NBC News, September 21, 2016, https://tinyurl.com/msuxpyny.

Four shots are heard: "Charlotte Police Release Dashcam Footage of Deadly Shooting," CBS Miami, September 25, 2016, https://tinyurl.com/4ay9wy9k.

We have tears: "Zianna Oliphant Speech," Tamu McPherson, June 1, 2020, YouTube video, https://tinyurl.com/2fd6v7zu.

Love seems with [Black people]: Thomas Jefferson, *Notes on the State of Virginia*, the Federalist Papers Project, 163, https://tinyurl.com/yc4b5t4y.

Half of them endorsed at least one myth: Linda Villarosa, "How False Beliefs in Physical Racial Difference Still Live in Medicine Today," *New York Times*, August 14, 2009, https://tinyurl.com/nmevezdh.

It was an affirmation of faith: James Cone, *The Spirituals and the Blues* (Ossining, NY: Orbis Books, 1972), 58.

Far from being songs of passive resignation: Cone, *The Spirituals and the Blues*, 35.

Officer Kimberly Potter was trying: Kelly Hayes, "Judge in Kim Potter Case Appears Emotional after Handing Down 2-Year Sentence," *Fox 13 Tampa Bay*, February 18, 2022, https://tinyurl.com/cuyh6tfz.

She took our baby boy: Lee Brown, "Kim Potter to Be Sentenced Friday in Daunte Wright Shooting Death," *New York Post*, February 18, 2022, https://tinyurl.com/5n86tv2k.

Free Black bodies: Kelly Brown Douglas, *Stand Your Ground: Black Bodies and the Justice of God* (Ossining, NY: Orbis Books, 2015), 86.

The "Individual Freedom" bill: Brendan Farrington, "Florida Could Shield Whites from 'Discomfort' of Racist Past," AP News, January 18, 2022, https://tinyurl.com/3rsb9th8.

Tell them they can be great: N. K. Jemisin, *The Fifth Season* (New York: Orbit Books, 2015), 76.

CHAPTER 7

I'm a crybaby: "Short Clip of Pastor Joel Osteen Breakdown Crying While Telling His Testimony of God's Blessings!," Jonathan DesVerney Gospel Channel, November 8, 2017, YouTube video, 10:17, https://tinyurl.com/yj7f7w68.

I feel very humbled: "Joel Osteen Cries on 60 Minutes," To God Be the Glory Forever, December 24, 2014, YouTube video, 2:41, https://tinyurl.com/mr3chade.

May well feel genuine: Ruby Hamad, *White Tears/Brown Scars* (New York: Catapult, 2020), 18.

Carry on the important work: Hamad, *White Tears/Brown Scars*, 52.

Kuchi must have wanted: Hamad, *White Tears/Brown Scars*, 59.

The absolute lack of threat: Luvvie Ajayi Jones, "How White Women Use Tears as a Weapon," Awesomely Luvvie, April 17, 2018, https://tinyurl.com/26735ebf.

Later, during the questioning: "Kavanaugh Accuser Testifies to Senate Committee (Full testimony)," CNN, September 27, 2017, YouTube video, 4:11:07, https://tinyurl.com/74r2aps9.

Little Liza, all of ten years old: "RAW FULL: Brett Kavanaugh Cries during Opening Statement," ABC15 Arizona, September 27, 2018, YouTube video, 44:42, https://tinyurl.com/24faecer.

A psychologically healthy adult: Steven Berglas, "Why Does John Boehner Cry So Much?," *Politico Magazine*, December 2, 2013, https://tinyurl.com/3djtnk97.

He'd ask if the person would be willing: Dylan Marron, *Conversations with People Who Hate Me* (New York: Atria Books, 2022), 23.

What the world needs: Howard Thurman, quoted in Gil Bailie, *Violence Unveiled: Humanity at the Crossroads* (New York: Crossroads Publishing, 1995), xv.

NOTES

CHAPTER 8

Gender ought not to be conceived: Judith Butler, *Gender Trouble: Feminism and the Subversion of Identity* (New York: Routledge, 1990), 143.

There is no reason to divide: Butler, *Gender Trouble*, 143.

Crying, and other signs of "failure": Jack Halberstam, *The Queer Art of Failure* (Durham, NC: Duke University Press, 2011), 3.

The lead chicken: Halberstam, *Queer Art of Failure*, 32.

It took Ronald Reagan another three years: Scott Calonic, "When AIDS Was Funny," *Vanity Fair*, December 1, 2015, https://tinyurl.com/2sn25anh.

I think that abstinence has been lacking: "President Reagan Delivers First Major Speech on AIDS Epidemic in 1987," ABC News, April 1, 1987, https://tinyurl.com/3xapa4wr.

A 2020 survey: Tim Fitzsimons, "40 percent of LGBTQ Youth 'Seriously Considered' Suicide in Past Year, Survey Finds," NBC News, July 15, 2020, https://tinyurl.com/dupvjspb.

Ballroom is a "social movement": Michael Roberson and Benji Hart, "The Ballroom Scene Has Long Offered Radical Freedoms for Black and Brown Queer People. Today, That Matters More Than Ever," *Time*, February 26, 2021, https://tinyurl.com/9vd2a4fr.

CHAPTER 9

Sadly, this can create a vicious cycle: N. M. Karakas and F. S. Dagli, "The Importance of Attachment in Infant and Influencing Factors," *Turkish Archives of Pediatrics* 54, no. 2 (2019): 76–81.

Children who were classified as secure: O. Gillrath, G. C. Karantzas, and R. C. Fraley, *Adult Attachment: A Concise Introduction to Theory and Research* (Amsterdam: Academic Press, 2016), 60.

I chose these two countries: "Employment: Length of Maternity Leave, Parental Leave, and Paid Father-Specific Leave," Organisation for Economic Co-operation and Development, https://tinyurl.com/9vd2a4fr.

In the domestic sphere: Shawn Flynn, *The Value of Ancient Children* (Oxford: Oxford University Press, 2018), 2.

Evidence suggests: A. A. Volk and J. A. Atkinson, "Infant and Child Death in the Human Environment of Evolutionary Adaptation," *Evolution and Human Behavior* 34 (2013): 182–92.

Education also consisted: Véronique Dasen, "Roman Childhood Revisited," in *Children in Antiquity: Perspectives and Experiences of Childhood in the Ancient*

Mediterranean, ed. L. A. Beaumont, M. Dillon, and N. Harrington (New York: Routledge, 2020), 111.

Whoever becomes humble: Matthew 18:4 NRSV.

Taking a day: Emma Goldberg, "The 37 Year-Olds Are Afraid of the 23-Year-Olds Who Work for Them," *New York Times,* October 28, 2021, https://tinyurl.com/55e3jvcy.

I've never really felt: Cheryl Teh, "Sen. Ron Johnson Says It's Not 'Society's Responsibility' to Care for 'Other People's Children' While Arguing against Childcare Subsidies for Working Parents," *Business Insider,* January 27, 2022, https://tinyurl.com/2p98dr9m.

Between 2005 and 2017: Emma Kauana Osorio and Emily Hyde, "The Rise of Anxiety and Depression among Young Adults in the United States," Ballard Brief, March 2021, https://tinyurl.com/5n6s3cwy.

That already elevated rate: Sarah Molano, "Youth Depression and Anxiety Doubled during the Pandemic, New Analysis Finds," CNN, August 10, 2021, https://tinyurl.com/53j8wbp7.

Gonzalez stood quietly: "Emma Gonzalez's Powerful March for Our Lives Speech in Full: Video," *Guardian,* March 24, 2018, https://tinyurl.com/4eypk78j.

People are suffering: "'How Dare You': This Is Greta Thunberg's Passionate Cry for Climate Action," ABC News (Australia), September 23, 2019, YouTube video, 4:44, https://tinyurl.com/z8m6zuz8.

If we truly felt the horror: K-12 School Shooting Database, Center for Homeland Defense and Security, https://tinyurl.com/4rzmsf4y.

A million species are threatened: "Media Release: Nature's Dangerous Decline 'Unprecedented'; Species Extinction Rates 'Accelerating,'" IPBES secretariat, https://tinyurl.com/mr34efpk.

CHAPTER 10

Don't let us get sick: Warren Zevon, "Don't Let Us Get Sick," track 12 on *Life'll Kill Ya,* Artemis Records, 2000.

Anything else: "How Many U.S. Deaths Are Caused by Poverty?," Columbia Public Health, July 5, 2011, https://tinyurl.com/bdctkkwt.

From the militarized equipment: Brittany Ramos DeBarros, Facebook, June 24, 2018, https://tinyurl.com/bddx2bfw.

Our war on terror: "President Bush Addresses the Nation," *Washington Post,* September 20, 2001, https://tinyurl.com/599ftfx9.

NOTES

Our idea of progress: Jenny Odell, *How to Do Nothing: Resisting the Attention Economy* (New York: Melville House Publishing, 2019), 191–92.

If grief can be a doorway: Robin Wall Kimmerer, *Braiding Sweetgrass: Indigenous Wisdom, Scientific Knowledge, and the Teachings of Plants* (Milwaukee: Milkweed Editions, 2015), 359.

This fragile but resilient hope: "America Needs to Admit How Racist It Is," The Problem with Jon Stewart Podcast with Bryan Stevenson, February 21, 2022, YouTube video, 53:10, https://tinyurl.com/2uj54dyw.